ECONOMIC THEORY AND THE CONSTRUCTION INDUSTRY

ECONOMIC THEORY AND THE CONSTRUCTION INDUSTRY

Patricia M. Hillebrandt, B.Sc.(Econ.), Ph.D.

Macmillan

First published 1974 by
THE MACMILLAN PRESS LTD
London and Basingstoke
Associated companies in New York
Dublin Melbourne Johannesburg and Madras

Distributed in the United States by HALSTED PRESS,
a Division of John Wiley & Sons, Inc., New York

SBN 333 14944 0

Printed in Great Britain by
RICHARD CLAY (THE CHAUCER PRESS), LTD.,
Bungay, Suffolk

To
MARY GREAVES
who made me write it

Contents

of taxation, effect of changes in the value of capital
assets. Shift in the demand curve. Total demand
curve. Price elasticity of demand. Income elasticity
of demand. Actual assessments of elasticities of
demand. Demand for new housing. Many different
housing markets. Housing to rent and housing to
purchase in the private sector. Forecasting the
demand for new housing: need-based forecasts,
forecasts of economic demand, extension of past
trends.

PART THREE: THE SUPPLY OF CONSTRUCTION

the derivation of average and marginal cost curves. Difference between traditional and industrialised construction. Uncertainty in work load. Non-reversibility of cost curves. Problem of accurate estimation of costs. Long-run costs. Iso-product curves. Effect of different technologies with different fixed costs. Problem of growth over time. Supply curve of the firm.

potential surprise, stimulus of various outcomes.
Stage II: Lowest worthwhile bid price: gambler
indifference map. Stage III: Towards winning a
profitable contract: likelihood of getting the job,
bidding indifference map, alternative objectives of
the firm. Value of the analysis.
Statistical Decision Theory:
Probability approach. Discussion of the probability
approach for Stage III analysis. A three-stage probability and utility approach.
Negotiation and Other Methods of Price Determination

Preface

The need for an analysis such as is presented in this book became clear to me while I was working as an economist in Richard Costain Ltd and later in the National Economic Development Office. My experience there convinced me that there were special problems of the construction industry in which application of the basic concepts of economics would be very helpful, but that this industry was in certain respects so different from others that the theory needed tailoring before meaningful application was profitable.

I had no opportunity to develop any theoretical approach to the construction industry until I was faced with the problem of introducing economics to students in the then Bartlett School of Architecture, now part of the School of Environmental Studies at University College, London.

More specifically, this book grew out of a one-year course given to M.Sc. students taking as one of their options the subject of building economics. These students came from many backgrounds: building, management, civil, mechanical or structural engineering, architecture, quantity surveying and economics. Most of them had considerable experience and some of them were themselves teachers in polytechnics or other institutions of higher education. They were taking the course in order to bring a new dimension into their thinking about the construction industry, and my problem was therefore to present economic theory in a way which would seem relevant to them and yet with sufficient depth for the students to be able to adopt its inherent logic as part of their own mental equipment which would be of value no matter with which aspect of construction they were later concerned. As the course developed, it became increasingly clear that there were many aspects of the industry which did not fit into classical economic theory, at least not without considerable adaptation. Slowly the theory that was taught began to be more specific to the construction industry.

Hence the book which emerges is one which aims to present economic theory to those concerned with construction and at the same time to interest economists in the special problems of the construction industry.

The book draws on the parts of economic theory which are useful and relevant for this purpose, concentrating on those areas where there is some analysis particularly appropriate to construction. In order that it shall be readable by non-economists without necessary reference to other texts, a general analysis of a situation is sometimes required. As a result, economists will find it possible to skip over Chapter 11 on market equilibrium and types of market situation. Non-economists who wish to delve deeper into the subject would be well advised to broaden their understanding by reading any good economic textbook, particularly for analysis of factors of production, general equilibrium and macro-economics, areas which this book hardly touches.

As far as I know, this is the first book to treat the construction industry from this point of view. It is, however, a field in which many questions remain unanswered. Some of them can be considered from theoretical standpoints alone, but most require applied research in the field to test the validity of hypotheses. It is hoped that this first tentative outline of the map will tempt researchers to study selected areas in greater detail.

Without the stimulus of discussion in seminars with successive groups of M.Sc. students, particularly those in the years 1971–2 and 1972–3, this book would not have been written. Many of my colleagues have given help on specific chapters. I should like to mention particularly Professor G. L. S. Shackle, who read part of the chapter on the price determination for a single project and gave help and encouragement for my use of his degree of potential surprise function. I am greatly indebted to the three friends and colleagues Professor Marian Bowley, Professor Duccio Turin and Mrs Margaret Bloom, who read and commented on the whole draft. As a result of their valuable criticisms and suggestions many amendments have been made and some parts completely redrafted. The responsibility for the deficiencies and errors which remain is mine alone.

P. M. H.

PART ONE

Introduction

1 The Nature of Construction Economics

SCOPE OF SUBJECT

Construction economics is a branch of general economics. It consists of the application of the techniques and expertise of economics to the study of the construction firm, the construction process and the construction industry. To understand the scope of the subject it is necessary firstly to know what economics is about, and secondly to ascertain why the construction industry deserves a special branch of the subject to itself.

Economics is essentially about choice of the way in which scarce resources are and ought to be allocated between all their possible uses. Robbins's (1935)[1] definition is: 'Economics is the science which studies human behaviour as a relationship between ends and scarce means which have alternative uses.' It is mostly about the choice of means to achieve ends and not of the ends themselves, although economists disagree among themselves on this. Robbins says: 'Economics is not concerned with ends as such.' Others, notably Boulding (1958),[2] have argued that economists are very closely concerned with the objectives of the economic system. Both are probably right since the objectives of the economic system, such as growth of national income, are not required as ultimate ends in themselves but as means to other objectives, for example an increase in the material comfort of the population, or a place in the counsels of the world's nations and in the world technological contest. The economist will be required to point out the implications of, for example, various rates of growth in investment for growth in consumption and to lay before the policy-makers (politicians rather than economists) the alternatives over time.

The situation in the study of the firm is similar, as will be seen when objectives of the firm are discussed. Most firms have a number of goals which will include, in different proportions, responsibility for welfare of workers, shareholders, customers and others. Sometimes these aims will conflict and then it will be not the economist but the policy-maker within the firm who must exercise his own judgement of values to determine the objectives of the firm over time. In most fields of the study of the economist, the final choice of ends is not his. His role is to state the implications of alternative choices. Historically, economists in their analysis of the firm take maximum profit as the end, but this is now being questioned as the most important objective. This is discussed in Chapter 8. Once the end has been established, the economist can advise on what action will be most likely to achieve the objective.

The resources in which the economist is interested are those which are scarce. Air is a vital resource for man. Without it he cannot live. Yet it is not usually a matter for study by economists because there is no shortage. As soon as there is a shortage an economic problem arises: for example, when man goes into space and air or oxygen becomes one of the many scarce resources to be taken on a space journey, or when because of pollution fresh air becomes scarce. In general, resources such as labour, land, buildings, machinery and raw materials are limited; hence they are of prime concern to economists.

METHODS OF SIMPLIFICATION

In order to study and analyse the workings of the complex and vast economic system, economists have had to develop various specialist skills and methods of simplification. Boulding (1958)[2] deals well with these skills. Here only a broad outline of methods of simplification will be given, leaving the nature of most of the techniques to emerge in later chapters as they are used.

One of the problems of economic analysis is the interdependence of the parts of the system so that a small change in one part will have repercussions, indeed waves of repercussions of decreasing intensity, throughout the rest of the system. Moreover, in a real-world situation change is taking place all the time and in different areas, and it is very difficult to know the cause of a change in one part of the system. One way of overcoming this problem is to consider the likely effect of a change in one variable, assuming that all other variables remain constant apart from the effect of the change. Thus the economist isolates one particular problem area, puts on blinkers so that he focuses his attention on this area alone and studies the effect of change on the assumption of 'other things being equal' (*ceteris paribus*). Boulding (1958)[2] describes this as 'the exploration of cross-sections in two or three dimensions of the *n*-dimensional model'.

Thus we can, for example, study the effect of the imposition of a training levy on construction firms, assuming in the first place that the levels of demand and of resource availability remain as before – both of which may be false in reality; but both assumptions are necessary to bring the problem down to a size with which the mind can cope.

The second major method of simplification is aggregation, i.e. lumping together a great mass of individual phenomena and looking at them as a whole. We are familiar with this method in national income accounting and even in the budget speech. Great use of this method was made by Keynes (1936).[3] By working with great blocks of income, consumption and investment, he was able sufficiently to simplify the system so that he could study the interrelationships of all the main parts of the system at once. Boulding (1958)[2] describes this method as 'squashing' the *n*-dimensional model rather than slicing it.*

The method of aggregation is used mostly in macro-economics, i.e. in a study of the operation of the whole system – the economy or the industry. The method of isolating a particular aspect of the economy or business unit for analysis, while assuming other parts to be stable, is used in studying the whole system as well as in studying any separate unit – the firm, the individual, i.e. in micro-economics. In both macro- and micro-economics and in using the method of aggregation and of isolation, the economist is establishing a model which is merely

---

*A useful pedagogic simplification is to consider the workings of a Robinson Crusoe economy where the method of aggregation is automatically used because the one person is synonymous with the community as a whole, but where the individual preferences still play an obvious part in the system. It has the additional advantage that there is no money in the system to complicate the thinking.

a simplified representation of the system or part of the system under analysis. Thus there are models of the national economy which are relatively sophisticated reconstructions of the expected relationships between various aspects of the economy such as balance of payments, rates of interest, consumption, investment, etc. An attempt has been made to use these models in national planning with not entirely satisfactory results, partly because of the difficulty of obtaining reliable relationships, and of forecasting exogenous variables. Such complex models are possible because of the availability of the computer which enables the implications of change in any one variable, e.g. a change in bank rate, on the whole system to be calculated relatively quickly. At the other extreme, the economist is using a model when he draws supply and demand curves for, say, wheat and uses them to study price.

RELATIONSHIP TO OTHER SUBJECTS

Economics increasingly overlaps with other subjects. Hague (1969)[4] relates management economics and operational research when he says that:

> Managerial economics is a fundamental academic subject which seeks to understand and to analyse the problems of business decision-taking. It is therefore an academic subject which underlies both operational research and the manager's day-to-day decisions.... Managerial economics is a background subject which both the line manager and the operational researcher must understand if they are to be successful. Operational research is a functional activity pursued by specialists within the firm. They seek to apply the basic principles of managerial economics and indeed of other academic disciplines like sociology, psychology, mathematics or statistics to business problems.

What applies to managerial economics applies equally to other forms of economics where the techniques of operational research can be used to solve a number of problems and above all to deal with more variables than can be achieved by the traditional economic approach. Using the results of the work of the operational researchers, the assumptions and analysis of economics will be refined and both subjects will benefit from each other. There is a fusion too between mathematics and statistics and economics. Management accounting is increasingly allowing the logic of economics to determine the way in which the information at its disposal should be collected, analysed and presented.

All economists need to rely on others for the raw data to which they can apply their theories and hence recommend action. They need to be told the technological limits within which there is an effective choice to be made. The construction economist needs the assistance of the designer, contractor, quantity surveyor, statistician and accountant, who will know more about various aspects of the construction process than he. The contribution of the economist so far to the problems of the construction industry has been small and mainly in the field of macro-economics of the construction industry and its place in the economy and in the economics of the firm. Other large areas which are or should be of concern to the economist are planning economics, design economics and site economics. Planning economics seems to have been approached more from the basic planning disciplines than from the economic disciplines. It includes cost–benefit analysis. At the moment the field of design economics is being investigated principally by quantity surveyors and architects with interests in broader issues, helped by operational researchers. There is scope for further study. Economists have barely touched this field, although it should be a subject in which they could give substantial help as it has all the ingredients of scarce resources, alternative uses and a wide area of choice. The reason for their small contribution is probably partly historical and partly that the technological constraints are extremely complex, the variables almost unlimited (skills of operational research are important here) and the aesthetic content important. Similarly, economists have not dealt substantially with site economics. The reasons for this are partly the opposite from those in design economics – namely that by the time the project reaches construction stage, the options still open in resource use are limited or, equally important, seen by contractors as being limited.

SPECIAL CHARACTERISTICS OF CONSTRUCTION

The construction industry has characteristics which, separately, are shared by other industries, but in combination appear in construction alone, making it worthy of separate treatment. These characteristics fall into four main groups: the physical nature of the product; the structure of the industry together with the organisation of the construction process; the determinants of demand; and the method of price determination.

The final product of the construction industry is large, heavy and expensive. It is required over a wide geographical area and is for the most part made specially to the requirements of each individual customer. A large part of the components of the product are manufactured elsewhere by other industries. It is largely these product characteristics which determine the structure of the industry, including the large number of dispersed contracting firms and the separation of design in professional offices from construction firms, which has such important repercussions. The nature of the product, together with the structure of the industry it encourages, also means that each contract often represents a large proportion of the work of a contractor in any year, causing substantial discontinuities in production functions. The work of the contracting part of the industry involves the assembly of a large variety of materials and components with implications for the relative importance of scarce resources.

Demand on the construction industry is for investment goods for which the ultimate use is:

(*a*) as a means to further production, e.g. factory building;

(*b*) as an addition to or improvement of the infrastructure of the economy, e.g. roads;

(*c*) as social investment, e.g. hospitals;

(*d*) as an investment good for direct enjoyment, e.g. housing.

The determinants of the demand for these categories of goods are different and need separate analysis. Moreover, government in some form, either central or local, is responsible for about half the demands on the industry and can affect directly or indirectly almost all the remainder. This preponderance of government influence, together with the investment nature of demand, means that demand tends to fluctuate particularly according to the state of the economy and the social and economic policies of the government, with consequent effects on the industry. This is discussed in Chapter 2.

There is some work, notably private speculative housing but also some commercial and industrial development, where the developer and the contractor are the same firm and hence where there is no overt price determination for the construction project. This probably accounts for a maximum of 15 per cent of the work of the industry (see Chapter 7). The price which the developer charges for the finished product, whether it is a dwelling or office for sale or an office or factory for rent, is influenced by many factors other than the price of the construction, such as the price of land, the price of capital and the system of taxation. It is therefore not covered in this book except in so far as it is necessary to the understanding of the determinants of demand on the industry (see Chapter 14).

Because of the physical nature of the product, the structure of the industry and the characteristics of demand, the method of price determination is usually a discrete process for each project and for each piece of work subcontracted, either by tendering or by some form of negotiation. General economic theory deals inadequately with this type of price determination.

In view of these unique characteristics of construction, there is a need for the development of new theoretical economic analysis, or at least for adaptation of existing theory, to assist in the understanding of the workings of the construction process, the construction industry and the construction firm. It is this which is the subject of this book.

2 Relation of the Construction Industry to the Economy

IMPORTANCE OF THREE CHARACTERISTICS

The importance of construction in the economy stems from three of its characteristics: firstly, its size; secondly, that it provides predominantly investment goods; and thirdly, that government is the client for a large part of its work.

The value of the final product of the industry in the United Kingdom, including materials, amounted in 1971 to about £5,600 million,[1] or nearly 12 per cent of the gross domestic product.[2] Even net output, i.e. excluding materials and supplies bought from other industries, amounted to 6 per cent of the gross domestic product.[2] New work undertaken by the industry accounted for about half of gross fixed-capital formation.[1, 2]

The total employment of the United Kingdom industry in 1971 was about 1·5 million persons, or about 6 per cent of the labour force.[1, 3] Even the repair and maintenance part of the industry has a labour force larger than those of agriculture and horticulture, of coal-mining, of shipbuilding and marine engineering, and of timber and furniture.[1, 3]

Not only in the United Kingdom but internationally construction is an important industry. Work undertaken by the Building Economics Research Unit at University College, London,[4] shows that in 1967 for poor countries with a *per capita* income range of $U.S.100–200, the net output of construction as a percentage of gross domestic product is between 3 and 6 per cent, while at the other extreme, for countries with a gross domestic *per capita* product of over $U.S.1,000, it ranges from 7 to 10 per cent. New construction accounts for between 45 and

60 per cent of gross fixed-capital formation in a majority of countries.

Construction is an investment-goods industry, i.e. the new products which it creates are wanted, not for their own sake, but on account of the goods or services which they can create or help to create. This is clear in the case of factory building, where the factory is used to produce other commodities. In a different way, however, it is also true of, say, a school building where the building is not required for its own sake, but as a place in which to produce education. Housing can be considered as the place where accommodation is produced. This stretches the argument rather far, however, and domestic housing, although it has many of the attributes of an investment good, is really directly consumed.

In another sense, too, the products of the construction industry are investment or capital goods, for their value is high in relation to the income of the purchaser. For the individual consumer, for example, the purchase of a house will usually entail the expenditure of several times his annual income. Similarly, the erection of a factory by a manufacturing firm will be a large expenditure in relation to the running costs of production and in relation to the annual income derived from it. Consequently the products of the construction industry, with the exception of repair and maintenance, are paid for out of capital, i.e. the purchasing power which has accrued in the past but not been used in the past. This capital may belong to the ultimate owner of the construction industry product or, more usually, may be borrowed from elsewhere.

By reason of the long life of construction products, the stock of products is large in relation to the annual production. Small fluctuations in the demand for the stock of buildings and works will have very large repercussions on the demand for the buildings and works created by the industry.

The importance of the public sector as a client of the industry also has far-reaching effects on the industry and the economy because government has a means of very direct control over the demand on the industry. In 1971, 35 per cent of the gross domestic fixed-capital formation in dwellings and other buildings and works was for local authorities, 10 per cent for central government and 11 per cent for public corporations, making the total 56 per cent in the public sector.[2] Some of this work is done by labour directly employed by these authorities, but, even of new work done by contractors, in 1971 the public sector accounted for 51 per cent.[1]

These three characteristics – size, investment-goods industry and dependence on government as a client – provide the key to the interrelationship between the industry and the economy. Size is important because changes in output of the construction industry affect the size of the national product both directly and indirectly, but it also means that what is happening to the construction industry must be a matter of national concern. It is much too big to ignore. It is also too important to ignore. As a provider of about half the country's fixed investment, if the output of the industry is down, total investment is down, and investment is of vital concern in considering the health of the nation. That it provides an investment good also means that it is very subject to fluctuations in demand, for most of its products will be required only if certain other factors are favourable, for example, the expected sales of the goods which the factory would produce; the availability of mortgages for house purchase; and the economic climate in which government takes decisions about the level of social services. For all these reasons, the moment of investment is a matter of choice and will be determined by a number of factors over which the construction industry has no control. Lastly, the dependence on government as a client means that government is able to reduce the demands on the industry by action on its own proposed projects, in addition to that indirect control it is able to exert on overall investment through control of credit and interest rates.

GOVERNMENT MANAGEMENT OF THE ECONOMY AND ITS EFFECT ON CONSTRUCTION

The mechanism of the way in which the industry interacts with the economy in the relatively short run of, say, five or ten years is best understood against a background of overall government policy *vis-à-vis* the economy.

The government, in managing the economy, attempts to achieve four main objectives: (i) solvency, i.e. the ability to pay its way abroad by balancing the payments made for goods and services of various types with the payments received for good and services: this is the balance-of-payments problem; (ii) an acceptable level of the employment of resources, particularly manpower: what is an acceptable level will vary over time and with political parties, but that more than a certain degree of unemployment is unacceptable is common policy; (iii) growth, i.e. the increase in the amount of goods and services which the country produces and is able to consume, in absolute terms and *per capita*, thus leading to a rise in the standard of living; (iv) control of inflation: until recently this would have been seen as a means to the achievement of the other objectives, but it is now a problem of such magnitude that it has virtually become an end in itself.

In most of the 1950s and 1960s the objective of solvency dominated economic policy in that it was the health of the balance of payments which determined how far other objectives of growth and full employment could be achieved. During a period of growth in incomes and in demand there is a tendency for imports to increase faster than exports. Imports increase because, with a rise in incomes, there is a direct consumer demand for imported goods and because before production of manufactured goods can be increased, raw materials, many of which are imported, must be obtained. The level of exports, on the other hand, is not closely related to the level of home incomes and consumer demand. Indeed, the fact that it is easy to sell goods in the home market may actually decrease the level of exports, which are more trouble to sell. The argument on the other side is that industry working at nearer full capacity can produce goods cheaper on average than one working at less than full capacity and therefore that the greater home demand should enable the goods to be more competitive in export markets. This factor does not seem strong enough over industry as a whole to alter the overall excess of imports over exports which arises with growth in the economy.

When the balance of payments is in imbalance, the government of whatever party has usually reacted by restricting growth and damping down demand. There are a number of ways in which it can do this: by acting on output, on employment, on incomes or on demand – for all these components of the economic scene are interrelated. A change in one automatically produces eventual changes in the others, because a decrease in employment causes a fall in incomes, which causes a fall in demand, which leads to a reduction in output, which in its turn again causes a drop in employment, and so on. Thus government can act to change the level of any one of these, knowing that it will have continuing repercussions on all the components of economic life. The imposition of Selective Employment Tax in 1966, for example, affected employment because employers found the price of labour had risen and hence reduced demand for it; and it affected incomes because some purchasing power had been taken from the economy. A decrease in building causes a fall in output which will cause decreases in employment in building and hence, other things being equal, falls in incomes and demand. Any tax on incomes reduces incomes and any tax on goods raises their prices and hence reduces demand for them. Government has in the post-war period used all these and other measures to regulate the economy. It is unfortunate for the construction industry that the ways in which it is easiest and least painful for the government to inject a new factor into the economic cycle have been found to be raising the rate of interest and restricting credit, so that it becomes more difficult and more expensive to borrow money; reducing purchasing power through an increase in taxation; and reducing its own spending, especially capital spending which is easier to postpone than current expenditure. The construction industry is affected directly or indirectly by all these measures.

An increase in interest rates raises the cost of capital projects at the same time as the reduction in purchasing power makes it less likely that profits from the capital expenditure would be as high as seemed likely before the measures were taken. This reduces industrial and commercial building, including that of nationalised industries. It also affects the rate at which local authorities may borrow and hence increases the cost of their schemes. It increases the cost and reduces the availability of funds for house purchase.

Not only does the rate of interest and supply of credit affect the demand on the construction industry, but it affects the firms in the construction industry, for they are very dependent on credit from banks and their material suppliers. In addition, those firms which have invested resources in speculative building may find their supply of finance in jeopardy, their costs of finance increased and the prospects of a good sale reduced.

Any reduction in purchasing power will similarly affect the construction industry. Manufacturers will anticipate a lower level of demand for their products and hence will postpone erection of new factories or offices. Service industries will be similarly pessimistic and will put off investment in shops, garages, hotels, etc. Again it will affect house purchase: potential buyers will have less income available for mortgage payments.

Lastly, the reduction by government of its own capital expenditure hits the construction industry particularly hard, as over half the new work done by the industry is for public-sector clients.

This description of the effects of 'squeezes' does not, however, do justice to the intricacies of their effects and the way in which each item of policy action will reinforce the others. The effect of a squeeze on building societies serves to illustrate these interrelationships. Parry Lewis (1965)[5] distinguishes four ways in which funds of building societies are affected. Firstly, the squeeze is usually imposed at a period of buoyant demand when there is an underlying inflationary tendency. In this situation investors will favour equities, the prices of which reflect somewhat the rate of inflation, rather than investment in building societies, where their capital keeps its face value but not its real value. Secondly, in a period of reduction of employment and incomes, there is a general reduction in saving. Thirdly, although in the long run share prices are expected to be fairly 'inflation-proof', in the short run, just after a squeeze is announced, share prices may fall, thus producing an additional incentive to invest for capital gain as well as a short-term high return on investment. Lastly, in a period of lower employment and incomes, borrowers will postpone repayment of their mortgage as long as possible, thus again reducing the funds available for new lending. All these factors produce a decline in funds available for lending which will cause societies to raise their interest paid at the same time as there is a reduction in the demand for mortgages, due to the higher interest rates and a reduction in incomes, and difficulties faced by speculative builders. It is not surprising that in a squeeze the level of private-sector house construction is particularly vulnerable.

EXTENT OF CONSTRUCTION INDUSTRY FLUCTUATIONS

The construction industry is at the receiving end of a large measure of government action in its attempts to regulate the economy. It is important to try to establish the extent of the effects on the industry. Graph (1) in Fig. 2.1 shows the fluctuations in the value of all work done by contractors and labour directly employed by public authorities. It is clear that until 1969 the alternate stop–go policies had not actually caused an absolute fall in the total value of work undertaken, and the figures for new work by contractors (graph (2)) were only slightly more peaked. In 1969 and 1970 the fall in the level of output took place entirely in housing. It is possible that on top of the fall in output due to the squeeze, there was also a long-term fall due to a gradual change in the balance of supply and demand. Thus the effect of the squeeze alone may not, even in 1969 and 1970, have been sufficient to cause an absolute fall in output. On graph (3) is shown the index of orders for new work by contractors. Here the fluctuations are much greater, and in 1964–6 and again in 1967–70 there were substantial falls in the level of new orders, both followed by a period of rapid expansion. Clearly, the more equable value of figures for work done is being smoothed by the long contract period in construction on big projects and also by the smoothness of the repair and maintenance output figures. It would be expected therefore that the firms which suffered most would be the medium-sized contracting firms which are too big to exist on repair and maintenance work and too small to reap the benefits of the smoothing effect of large contracts. Unfortunately statistics to give detailed support to this thesis are not available. The statistics of value of output by size of firm do not show how many firms have moved from one size group to another. In a period of rapid expansion firms would move into a higher category and return in less buoyant times. However, the smaller the category considered, the greater the fluctuations which would be expected. This shows up in the statistics of new orders where, for example, there was in the period 1960–3[6] a dip in

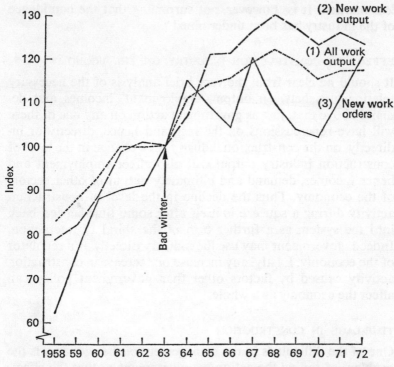

FIG. 2.1. Fluctuations in orders and output (1963 = 100)

Definitions and sources:

(1) Output of all work by contractors and by operatives directly employed by the public sector.
(2) Output of new work by contractors.
(3) Orders for new work by contractors.

All from Ministry of Public Building and Works, *Bulletin of Construction Statistics, 1969*, and Department of the Environment, *Housing and Construction Statistics*, no. 3, 3rd qtr. 1972. (1972 figures provisional.)

orders for private housing, private industrial and private non-industrial work which did not show up in the total figures. Similarly, greater fluctuations appear in the regional figures and in the figures by size of contract (both available only from the mid-1960s) than in the national figures.[1, 6] All this leads to the general conclusion that individual firms of contractors will have been quite substantially affected by the fluctuations due to stop–go, although the effect over the industry as a whole was less marked. It is, however, not surprising that the confidence of the industry has been undermined.

EFFECT OF CONSTRUCTION INDUSTRY ON THE ECONOMY

It should be clear from the very brief analysis of the necessary relationships between output, employment, incomes and demand above that, just as government action on any one of these will have repercussions on the rest, and hence, directly or indirectly, on the construction industry, so a change in the level of construction industry output will also affect employment and hence incomes, demand and ultimately output of other sectors of the economy. Thus the decline in the level of construction activity during a squeeze is itself after some time-lag fed back into the system as a further turn of the spiral of interaction. Indeed, government may use the industry directly as a regulator of the economy. Lastly, any increase or decrease in construction activity caused by factors other than government policy can affect the economy as a whole.

TIME-LAGS IN CONSTRUCTION

One of the difficulties in the management of the economy is the problem of timing the action by government so that the effects of the action occur at the correct time to achieve the desired objective. The lags in the construction process tend to be long and very variable. If government reduces its capital expenditure programme it will not normally make any cuts to the projects on which construction has actually started. The build-up of the work load on a contract is slow at first, then it increases very rapidly and towards the end of the project tails off again. This pattern is similar for large projects and for small projects with the allotted duration of each project. Thus if large projects are postponed, the reduction of the work load from what it would have been had the projects been allowed to continue would be very small for some months. If smaller projects were cancelled, the effect would be quicker but still with an initial slow effect. Later in the contract period – perhaps a year or so later – the reduction in work load would be substantial. The difficulty therefore about making any use of construction projects to depress demand on the economy is that, unless the government can foresee problems very far in advance, the effect will be too slow to be useful at the beginning of the period and the major effect will come much later, perhaps at a time when the contrary effect is clearly required. There is a further problem which affects the internal pressures on the resources of the industry, namely that cancellation of projects can for some time relieve pressure only on the skills and materials used at the beginning of projects. If it is, say, electricians who are in short supply, then alteration in the demands on the industry will have no effect for some months since electricians are employed mostly at the end of any project.

At the same time, because the total process of construction from the moment the client briefs his professional adviser to the completion of the project is a long one spanning many different occupations and skills, a sudden halt to starts of projects followed by their later commencement all together leads to disruption of the whole design process as well as of the work done on site. It is this disruption about which the industry particularly complains because it is felt that its situation is not understood. It is argued elsewhere[7] that the oscillations of demand probably have some desirable effects, such as more rapid technological change, which at least partly offset the serious effects of the disincentive to invest in plant and skills. However, very large fluctuations are probably damaging to the overall efficiency of the industry.

CONSTRUCTION INDUSTRY AS A REGULATOR

In spite of the damage to efficiency of sudden stops and starts in its work load, because of its size and importance, the construction industry is a tempting regulator and successive governments are accused of using the construction industry as a regulator of the economy. With one or possibly two exceptions, however, there is no evidence that in the post-war period governments have deliberately used the construction industry as a direct regulator.* They have rather applied general controls on credit and demand and on their own spending, and the construction industry happens, by reason of the three characteristics mentioned at the beginning of this chapter, to have been affected

* This passage was written before the measures of December 1973.

more, or more obviously, than some other industries by these measures. On the other hand there are industries which suffer more, notably the motor industry, for the same or similar reasons.

One possible exception to this general rule was the Building Control Bill introduced in May 1966 (it had been previously introduced in late 1965 but did not then go through on account of the general election). This provided for the licensing of private projects above a certain value other than housing and industrial construction. It was intended that the controls should be used to even out the fluctuations in the construction industry and, at the time the Bill was originally conceived in 1965, the industry was working very near to the limit of its capacity. The government was presumably afraid that an even higher load would send up costs without increasing output and that it might be the more essential projects which were delayed. By the time the Bill was enacted, however, the pressure on the industry had already begun to ease, no doubt partly owing to the high interest rates from the preceding November, and the Act came too late. It is not known how much effect it had on the industry's load because there may have been many projects which would have gone forward but which were daunted by the prospect of obtaining a licence. It was never used to bite as hard as might have originally been intended and it has been in cold storage since 1968. The curiosity of the Act is that at least in public it was declared to be necessary to regulate the industry for the industry's own good and not as a regulator of the economy.

The first post-war case of the construction industry being deliberately and openly used as a regulator of the economy came in 1971, when the government authorised a two-year emergency public works programme for development and intermediate areas, with the stated purpose of countering the growing level of unemployment. Perhaps this policy was presented in this way simply because the industry is unlikely to object to its use as an upward regulator, while it would object violently to a downward regulator. The cuts in public spending announced in May 1973 had a high construction component and in addition were unaccompanied by other measures, so that it is debatable whether in this instance construction was used as a direct regulator.

LONG-TERM CHANGES IN CONSTRUCTION ACTIVITY

The level of construction activity can and does change for reasons other than government action. Indeed, because it is an investment industry the demand for its products is related to the *rate* of growth of the final consumer product rather than the absolute level, and this in itself leads to large fluctuations over time (see Chapter 5).

Parry Lewis (1965),[5] in a painstaking analysis of building cycles in Britain from 1700, has found that there are distinct long-term fluctuations in construction activity, often regional in character, and finds the 'key ... in population, credit and shocks....' The shocks he has in mind are, for example, bad harvests or war, which will have repercussions on the natural increase in population, on migration, etc. They will also affect the monetary sector, often through the balance of payments. Population and credit as exogenous variables can be taken into account in making long-term forecasts of construction activity, for example of housing and education, but shocks cannot by their very nature be taken into consideration in the forecasting process. Yet clearly their effect on construction and the effect of construction on the economy through the level of total production and through the demand for money can be as important as the effect of the economy on the construction industry.

It may be possible by some form of national planning and management of the economy to offset some of the undesirable interactions between the industry and the economy, but the history of national planning in the 1960s does not give great encouragement to this hope. Meanwhile our understanding of the interaction can be increased by continued study of the relationships and by attempts to predict future developments.

FUTURE OUTLOOK

The construction industry has made successive representations to government, asking sometimes for an end to stop–go or sometimes for an alleviation of its effects.

There does not, however, appear any likelihood that there will be an end to fluctuations of the demands on the construction industry. In the first place, the policy objectives of government, of solvency, full employment and growth, have not been found to be simultaneously realisable, and now that the problem of inflation looms large, its control has become an additional goal of government economic management. With these important objectives in jeopardy, it seems unlikely that government will flinch from allowing some fluctuation in construction activity if by so doing it seems to bring the attainment of these overriding objectives any closer. Nor would it be in the long-term interest of the construction industry were it to do so, for it has been shown that the health of the industry is inextricably mixed up with the health of the economy.

Secondly, the analysis of Parry Lewis (1965)[5] leads to an expectation that there will be fluctuations in the level of construction demand brought about by factors outside the control of government. Since, as is shown in Chapter 6, much of the demand for the public-sector projects is dependent on judgements of their social desirability, and since there is usually a 'pool' of desirable projects awaiting approval, it should be possible for government to offset some of the fluctuations in demand in other sectors by alterations in its own programmes – always provided that this did not conflict with the economic objectives mentioned above. It seems unlikely however, that major adjustments could be made without some fluctuation in the demand on the industry.

It is suggested that the industry would be wise to accept that it is subject to fluctuations and that both it and government must find ways to alleviate some of the undesirable effects of fluctuations. There are several ways in which this can be done. The first is that as much knowledge as possible should be obtained on the likely changes in demand. This implies forecasting the demands on the industry some years ahead. A first attempt at such forecasts has already been made[8] and the methodology will slowly be improved. That such forecasts have been made and have been found so far to accord reasonably with reality should help to give the industry confidence in its future and in its power to know its future. These forecasts may be useful in the planning of measures to even out the level of demand on the industry.

Secondly, the capacity of the construction industry itself

must be studied and monitored to ensure that it is likely to be able to meet the demands upon it. A methodology by which this might be done is suggested elsewhere.[7]

Thirdly, government should consider whether it can give more forward knowledge to the industry, not only of the overall load of work, but of detailed programmes and future individual projects. There is the difficulty that the government must reserve the right to cancel programmes or amend them, but this could surely be overcome by stating the priorities to be given to each project.

Lastly, more should be done to consider the effect of various ways of letting work to the industry, against a background of fluctuations in demand. Too little is known of the effect on the efficiency of firms of various sizes and types of specialisms of fluctuations in their work load.

3 Some Basic Concepts in Economics

There are some concepts used by economists in the whole of micro-economics which it is appropriate should be explained at the outset, in order that the flow of the argument in later chapters is not interrupted by a digression to explain their meaning, and also so that they can be used before the stage of the main exposition of their use is reached. First, the meaning of the terms 'industry' and 'market' as they apply to construction are considered. There follows a discussion of various types of cost and then of price, profit, the nature of marginal analysis and the concepts of supply and demand. For further definitions of terms, the reader is referred to the index where page references to definitions and explanations of the use of terms are shown in heavy type.

NATURE OF THE CONSTRUCTION INDUSTRY AND OF
CONSTRUCTION MARKETS

Construction may be regarded as one industry whose total produce is durable buildings and works. It is the contracting part of the industry which undertakes to organise, move and assemble the various materials and component parts so that they form a composite whole of a building or other work. The product which the contracting industry is providing is basically the service of moving earth and material, of assembling and managing the whole process. To the extent that the service given and the management supplied are similar through various building types, the industry can be regarded as one industry. The service and management will, however, vary according to the technical process involved, and to this extent there is not one industry but many sub-industries which may be regarded as coming under the umbrella of the main industry concept.

Some guide to the types of such sub-industries may be obtained from the list of twenty-two separate trades used by the Department of the Environment in its statistics.[1] There are many other subdivisions which could be regarded as desirable, including many divided not only by specialism but also by type of work, such as schools or roads. For some specialisms such as painting the actual type of building constructed is relatively unimportant, whereas for some others such as heating and ventilating or constructional engineering the nature of the work will vary considerably with the type of project. When considering the degree of competition it is, however, not even the industry or sub-industry which is relevant, but the market in which a group of firms, whose products are more or less substitutes for each other, operates. A market, in the economist's sense, means any organisation whereby the buyers and sellers of a particular commodity are kept in close touch with each other and are able to determine the price of the commodity. Commodity in the construction industry sense means a package of services which are more or less close substitutes for each other and are regarded by buyers and sellers as being so. The organisation required may be of any degree of formality. It may be at one extreme of the type of the stock exchange where price determination takes place only by a select list of buyers and sellers in a distinct geographical location, or it may, as in construction, mean the whole mechanism of the selection of the contractor and the fixing of the price at which the services he has to offer will be provided. The nature and the size of these construction industry markets and the factors which determine their limits need to be considered in some detail.

Size of contract is clearly a major determinant of the number of firms who can undertake work. A large contract requires more of all inputs than a small contract, and only some of the total number of contractors in the country have these inputs available to them. Capital is particularly important in this connection.

Complexity of contract is another determinant of the potential competitors. A complicated building can be constructed only by firms having control over the technical expertise required. This technical expertise has many components: for example, the variety and depth of technical skills, and the level of technology of the materials and processes. It should theoretically be possible to measure the degree of complexity, although the practical difficulties are great. Probably the nearest readily available approximation is cost per square metre for building of a given type. Clearly, if complexity and size are combined, the expected proportion of firms within the sub-industry who would in principle be interested in work of that type would be lower.

The idea of complexity would be of help in understanding the effect of location on the number of firms interested. The reason why firms do not go outside a certain geographical area of operation is that the costs in terms of transport of materials, plant and men become excessive in relation to total costs. If, however, the building is very complex, other things being equal, the cost per square metre is likely to be large and the costs of transport decrease in relation to the total costs of the project. Size also has an effect. For small projects some distance away it would not be economical to set up a local recruitment office, hostels, etc., because their fixed cost would be too high in relation to the total cost of a project. For large projects, however, the fixed costs could be spread over a large turnover and the existence of a local office for the project would enable the variable costs of transport and control to be substantially reduced. These are of course just two of the factors affecting a contractor's decision on the geographical range of operations. It is hoped that current research* will throw light on the relative importance of other factors.

Thus the larger and more complicated the contract, the lower the expected proportion of firms in the sub-industry who would be interested, but this effect is partly offset by the proportion of transport costs of these projects being relatively low, so that the effective catchment area is increased. Diagrammatically, the position is shown in Fig. 3.1. To some extent the relationships between the client and the firm determine which markets a firm can operate in. A firm which grows big may lose clients for small work because they can no longer be sure of having the personal attention of the managing director, or because they

*Project by the Building Economics Research Unit, University College, London.

assume that the big firm will charge too high a price on account of its higher overheads.

The markets in the construction industry should therefore be defined in terms of the total demand for a particular identifiable service (which is not a close substitute for other services

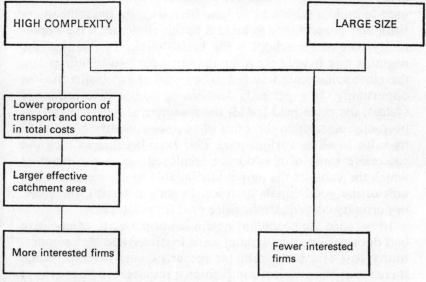

FIG. 3.1. Direct and indirect effects of complexity and size

outside this market) of a certain degree of complexity and size of contract and in a geographical area which may be covered, without undue increases in costs, by firms likely to be capable of undertaking work of that type. The total number of firms interested in work of this type will be referred to as being in a particular market.

TYPES OF COST

It follows from the nature of economics, as a subject dealing with scarce resources and their use to maximise a benefit of some kind, that the use of a resource for one purpose implies its withdrawal from another purpose. The cost of using a resource in use A is the lost opportunity of its employment in B. Hence the real cost of using the resource in A is the lost opportunity or 'opportunity cost'.

As an example, consider the opportunity cost of capital. If money capital is invested in a painting business the opportunity cost of its use there is the return which could be obtained on that capital with the same risk in another industry – say plant hire or even watchmaking. Similarly, if all the resources used to build a school could have been used (in the same quantities and proportions) to build a health clinic, then the opportunity cost of the school is the health clinic. In practice, the resource mix is unlikely to be the same for two buildings and therefore some other way has to be found of expressing the lost opportunity. In a perfectly functioning competitive economic system, the price paid for all the resources is equal to the opportunity cost, since the price of each commodity is equal to its value in all its various uses. This is so because in each use successive units of a good are employed up to the point at which the value of the output attributable to the use of the last unit of the good equals its price. In such a system, therefore, opportunity cost equals the price paid for resources.

In practice the economic system is not perfectly competitive and does not function without some frictions, and hence opportunity cost and price paid for resources may diverge. When there is less than perfect competition a resource may not always be used up to the point at which the value of the output attributable to the use of the last unit equals price, and this is one source of error in the use of price as a measure of real cost. Probably even more important is that prices do not respond immediately to the pressures of supply and demand. This 'stickiness' of prices means that, for example, the price of skilled manpower, i.e. the wage rate, may not equate demand and supply so that at the ruling price there is some shortfall in supply and the process of allocation of supply has to be done by some other method in addition to price. This may be rationing, first come first served, or perhaps by some non-money or at least non-wage inducements to labour to satisfy certain types of demand. This 'stickiness' in wages is due to a number of factors. Changes in wages for a skill tend to be related to wages in other industries and changes in the cost of living, and these factors exert a restraining influence on the speedy adjustment of wage rates to scarcity. Trade union influence, too, largely because it involves negotiating through elaborate institutional machinery, tends at times to be a delaying factor in adjustment.

Two other major cost concepts are long-term costs and short-term costs. Long and short term are not fixed periods of time but vary according to the matter under consideration. In general, the short term is a period so short that there are certain factors which cannot be altered. Thus the costs of producing additional output of sheet glass from an old plant with much maintenance requirement and substantial labour and material cost will be high. The cost of producing additional output of sheet glass from a new, technically efficient plant may be much lower. But the new plant would take, say, five years to build. In the short run (five years in this case) the costs are high, in the long run low.

A further pair of costs are social costs and private costs. Social costs are costs to the community; private costs are costs to the individual or group of individuals. The nature of these and other costs will be illustrated in some detail by an exploration of the relative costs of industrialised and traditional housing between the early 1960s and the early 1970s.

DIVERGENCE OF MONEY COST FROM LONG-TERM OPPORTUNITY COST

In the early 1960s the price of a dwelling built by industrialised methods, which use more capital and less labour than traditional methods, was higher than the price of a dwelling built by traditional methods. The exception was high-rise construction over five storeys where the industrialised was cheaper than traditional. At this time the amount of industrialised construction was relatively small, although a boom was just beginning.

Observers of the industry in this period were of the opinion that the relative prices at this time were not completely representative of the real costs or opportunity costs because of the 'stickiness' of wage rates. There was already a shortage of skilled manpower which was not completely reflected in wage rates. Moreover, it was expected that in the long run the costs of industrialised construction would fall as demand increased owing to the spreading of the high initial capital costs over a larger production and because of the reduction of costs due to the increased experience with this new technology. Thus short-term and long-term costs diverged.

The relative prices of goods reflect the situation at the time and do not take account of the forecasts of demand and resource availability. It was anticipated that total housing output would rise very substantially during the 1960s and that the supply of manpower would not increase, thus making any system which economised in manpower desirable in the long term. It was expected therefore that the money costs would come to reflect the shortage of manpower and therefore that ultimately the industrialised methods which employed relatively little manpower would become cheaper than traditional building.

In the event many of the anticipations were correct, although there were other factors, which would have been difficult to forecast, which confounded some of the expectations. The demand for industrialised dwellings did rise, as shown by the number started, from 28,000 in 1964 to a peak in 1967 of 66,000, but by 1971 they had fallen to below the 1964 level at 24,000,[2] partly owing to a reaction against high-rise building following the collapse of the block of flats, Ronan Point, and to policy decisions to decrease public authority building. However, only a handful of the hundred or so systems really flourished and there is no definite evidence of any substantial fall in costs on account of the rise in the number of industrialised dwellings.

Similarly, evidence on the effect on costs of learning and experience in the production of industrialised dwellings is slight except that, clearly, those which survived the decade must have been producing with much lower risks than at the beginning of the period. There is evidence (Bishop, 1965)[3] that the erection time of each gang decreases rapidly with experience but over a relatively short period, and there is no information on whether there has been a substantial change over the decade.

There are no statistics of wages or earnings of operatives employed in industrialised construction, and hence it is not known whether they moved in the same way as for all skilled construction workers. In the period 1963–8 earnings rose sharply in construction as a whole and at a marginally faster rate than in other main industries. However, there was still a serious shortage of craft labour from June 1963 to June 1966 as measured by unfilled vacancies.[4] Thus by 1967 money costs and real costs should have moved slightly closer together. The position was reversed in the late 1960s and early 1970s with craft labour losing some of the relative benefits it had gained in hourly earnings over other industries, and with increasing unemployment of skilled men.[4] At the same time there was a decrease in system building,[2] but how far one can claim a cause-and-effect relationship is doubtful.

It is probable that the rise in the real cost of labour after taking account of productivity was higher than that of other inputs. A definite assessment is difficult largely because of the problem (partly due to the unknown number of self-employed) of correcting the index of wages for productivity increases to obtain an index of the real cost of labour. Even then the costs of those engaged on industrialised building may not have been typical. Capital-goods prices[5] and rates of interest[6] over the period 1963–71 rose by about 40 per cent, materials for house-building[4] by about 45 per cent, labour costs[7] by about 90 per cent and net output per head, estimated on the basis of the discussion in the Reddaway Report on the effects of S.E.T. (1973),[8] by about 25 per cent, so it does seem likely that the rise in the real cost of labour (at around 65 per cent) was greater than that of other inputs, even allowing for doubts on the validity of the indices.

As a result of all the factors operating, the tender prices of industrialised dwellings became lower than the prices of traditional dwellings. Thus, using statistics corrected for area of dwelling,* the tender prices for industrialised houses and bungalows in 1964 were 10 per cent higher than for traditional building, but by 1971 the advantage had moved to industrialised dwellings and it was traditional which were more expensive by 5 per cent. In 1964 flats of two to four storeys were 8

*The method used is that developed by Reiners (1957)[9] and used and discussed by Stone (1970).[10] The statistics used are those of floor area and cost of construction; industrialised and traditional building; tenders approved for local authorities, England and Wales. They are now collected and published by the Department of the Environment[1] and were previously published by the Ministry of Housing and Local Government.[2]

per cent more expensive by industrialised methods; in 1971 their price was 9 per cent higher by traditional methods. Flats in five storeys or more were cheaper by industrialised methods than traditional even in 1964 and were still cheaper in 1971. Their percentage advantage increased over the period from 3 per cent to 13 per cent. The 1971 figure is, however, based on very few dwellings, and in the one year of 1970, when there were also relatively few dwellings, the cost advantage was actually the other way. The difficulty in interpreting these figures is that they are what the contractors actually quoted for the construction and do not therefore necessarily represent costs over the period. If profit levels for industrialised dwellings fell substantially from 1964 to 1971, this could have accounted for at least some of the changes, although cost changes undoubtedly also played their part.

SOCIAL COSTS AND PRIVATE COSTS

The difference between social costs and private costs is well shown by the example of industrialised housing.

The client of the industry is in the private sector a property developer or speculative builder, both of whom sell to purchasers of single dwellings for their occupation. In the public sector the client is one of the many local housing authorities, a housing association, a new town or a government department. With the exception of a few very large local authorities in the conurbations and some government departments and new towns, this client – public or private – is interested in one or a relatively small number of houses now.* He is not therefore interested in the possible long-term reduction in the costs of industrialised building which might accrue if the market is supported and enlarged. Nor is he much concerned with schools, hospitals or roads, for he is not responsible for building them. His private cost therefore tends to equal the short-term money cost, and on this basis in the early 1960s the traditional house had the advantage.

Society, on the other hand, has a continuing responsibility

*In 1971, 6·4 per cent of the number of new orders for public housing and none of those for private housing were in schemes valued at over £500,000.[11]

for housing and for the provision of many other facilities involving the use of construction industry resources. It is therefore concerned with the long term and with alternative uses of resources. Social cost tends to equal long-term opportunity cost.

It is also important for society to consider the possible effects on the economy at large of allowing the price mechanism to make the adjustment in the supply and demand situation for labour. If the industry raises the price at which it buys skilled labour, this will have the effect of making it beneficial to economise in labour, but because it takes a long time to train a skilled craftsman, it will not for some years substantially increase the supply. Meanwhile the higher price of labour will be passed on to clients in a higher cost of housing with ultimately inflationary results.

On the other hand if the price of labour does not rise and the clients of the industry do not try and economise in it by using less labour-intensive methods, then some housing will simply not get built in the time expected. In these circumstances therefore the social cost of not using labour-saving methods may be considerably higher than the private cost.

Government at the time of the boom in industrialised building exhorted clients of the industry to use industrialised methods, but much of the action by government (e.g. the establishment of the National Building Agency) came too late to avoid the industry running into serious resource scarcities in 1964–5, and by the time their exhortations and measures had taken effect they were no longer so necessary. An alternative policy would have been to take measures to bring the private money costs of industrialised and traditional building nearer to the social long-term costs by a tax or subsidy system – perhaps decreasing over, say, the ten-year period to take account of the anticipated long-term movement of costs.

SUNK COSTS

Because the economist is concerned with the value of a resource in an alternative situation, if the resource no longer has an alternative use, i.e. if it has no opportunity cost, it ought not to be considered in the decision-making process. If, for example, a lot of research has been devoted to developing a particular item of machinery and it appears that the likelihood of success is very small, in considering whether to continue with the research or not the labour which has been spent in the past is irrelevant because it now has no opportunity cost. All that is relevant is the cost of the resources (including opportunity cost) to be spent in the future compared with the benefits likely to be derived from them. Such costs incurred in the past, and which cannot now be altered, are 'sunk costs'. They may be capital costs or variable costs, e.g. a highly specific building which has no resale value or an amount of manpower. Not all costs incurred in the past are sunk costs. Past expenditure on a factory, for example, may be partly offset by the sale of the factory. The price received will be the opportunity cost of keeping it in its present use.

PRICE

Price is the rate at which exchange may or does take place and it applies to all resources and factors of production; thus the price of wheat is so many pounds a ton, the price of labour is wages, the price of capital is interest. Price is usually expressed in money terms, but in a barter economy where there is no money there is also a price of, for example, grain in terms of knives.

Price has an important part to play in the workings of the economic system as the mechanism which balances supply and demand.

PROFIT

Profit is the revenue obtained by a firm in excess of costs of that firm. Since costs in the economic sense include a normal return on capital and on entrepreneurial ability, i.e. a return sufficient to keep the capital and entrepreneur in the industry, firms can stay in business making no profit in the economist's sense (although not in the accountant's sense).

MARGINAL ANALYSIS

The marginal cost is a type of cost foreign to many disciplines such as old-fashioned financial accounting, although not to management accounting. It is very important for economic analysis, for economists ask the question: 'What difference will it make to the total cost if production is increased?' The difference in the total is the marginal cost.

The concern with the marginal differences goes right through economic analysis, and marginal cost is just one of many marginal concepts used by the economist. He also asks the questions: 'What will be the difference in my total satisfaction if I have another £10 of income per annum? What will be the increase in the revenue from sales if I increase my sales by, say, 20 units?' He asks similar questions about changes to that total as a result of falls in sales, decreases in production, etc. Thus for any projected change he is able to assess the decrease in total benefit on the one hand, and the increase in total benefit on the other hand, and hence whether the final benefit is larger or smaller than it would have been without the change. If he assesses this marginal change for very small changes in the variable, he can find his optimum position.

The presentation of marginal analysis, as it is called, may be done graphically, as in this book, or by differential calculus, which gives more accurate results and can be used for a greater number of variables. The latter does, however, require a familiarity with differential calculus and a mathematical approach and way of thinking not assumed in this book.

DEMAND AND SUPPLY

A detailed analysis of the nature of demand and supply forms the major part of this book. The two concepts are, however, so closely interlinked that it is necessary to refer to supply curves in the demand section and hence some brief explanation is appropriate here.

The amount of any commmodity demanded at various price levels can be expressed graphically as in Fig. 3.2 below, where the demand curve for a commodity is line *AB*, such that the lower the price, the greater the amount demanded. *CD* is the supply curve for the same commodity, showing that the lower the price the less will be the amount on offer. The curves cut each other at *E*. At price *OF* the amount demanded is *OG* and the amount which is on offer or supply is also *OG*. *E* is the

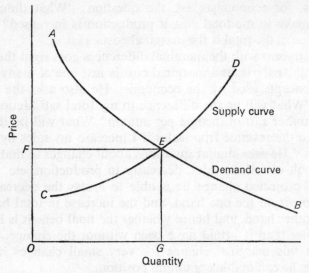

FIG. 3.2. Demand and supply curves

point of equilibrium and the point at which exchange will take place. If the price were greater than *OF*, more would be on offer than demanded and suppliers would tend to lower their price until the amount demanded equalled the amount they wanted to sell; while if the price were less than *OF*, the amount demanded would be greater than the amount on offer and the would-be purchasers would be willing to pay more up to a price of *OF* at which the demands at that price were met by the supply at that price.

PART TWO

The Demands on the
Construction Industry

4 Demand for Housing

Many products of the construction industry are built for the collective enjoyment or benefit of a large group of persons, e.g. schools and reservoirs, and the purchase of the service or benefit may be made by a group other than the users. These are the social-type goods discussed in Chapter 6. Another group of products is desired because they enable some benefit to be produced, e.g. industrial and commercial building discussed in Chapter 5. The construction of housing, however, enables a benefit to be available for direct consumption. In a minority of cases the client of the industry is the user, as in privately commissioned housing. Most housing, however, is either produced by a private developer in advance of orders by users or by a public authority for renting (or sale) to users. The private developer is known as a speculative builder – speculative in the sense that there is uncertainty as to whether the dwelling will be sold. In this sense at least a large part of the output of manufacturing industry is speculative. The manufacturer of toothbrushes does not know his clients when he produces the brushes. However, the sheer size of the purchase of a house and the fact that it is a postponable capital transaction renders speculative housing a more uncertain business than the manufacture of toothbrushes. The public authority normally constructs dwellings only when there is a clear demand at the price at which it is prepared to let them. This price may be lower than the market price and contain an element of subsidy, whereas the private builder will usually sell at the market price and will produce dwellings only when he anticipates that he will make a profit. In spite of the differences between the various types of client, all are dependent on the consumer's assessment of the desirability of housing compared with all the other goods and services he could buy with his available resources and hence on how much he is prepared to buy at various prices. In the Appendix the underlying basis of consumer demand is analysed with the help of indifference curves. In this chapter it is assumed that the individual consumer has decided how much housing he is prepared to purchase at various prices.

INDIVIDUAL'S DEMAND CURVE FOR HOUSING

In Fig. 4.1 on the horizontal axis is measured the quantity of housing in notional units per annum. On the vertical axis is the price of these notional housing units. Then the demand curve

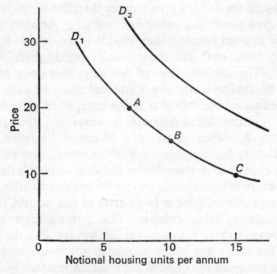

FIG. 4.1. The demand curve of the individual

for an individual for housing units will take the approximate form of, say, D_1. The curve slopes downwards to the right and is convex to the origin, since the more units of housing the individual has, the less he values further units of housing. Thus with a price of 20 the individual will demand 7 units of housing, as shown by point *A*, at a price of 15 he will demand 10 units (point *B*), and at a price 10 he will demand 15 units (point *C*).

CONCEPT OF NOTIONAL UNITS OF HOUSING

The measurement of housing in terms of notional units of housing is a conceptual tool. Housing is not homogeneous. Any system by which one tries to add up the standards of light, space, plumbing, electricity, aesthetics – to mention only a few – must be based on assessments of their relative values which are matters of opinion. The most practical method of arriving at the relative value of various amenities is to express them all in money values, but this is of little assistance for present purposes, as it is often the very money values (or prices) which are under study. Biggeri (1973)[1] has suggested a methodology for a survey of dwelling quality in Italy using a number of features of a dwelling each to be appraised on a system of penalty points. Duncan (1971)[2] has also undertaken a study of the problems of measuring the quality of housing and of its environment. He examines the existing sources of data on the condition of housing and describes work on the preparation of indices of the physical condition of housing. He is not, however, searching primarily for a method of counting equivalent units of housing, but his work is a useful study of the factors which affect the weighting of the unit and how they might be assessed. Economists who have worked on housing and tried to assess elasticities of demand (see below) have been forced to consider what unit they are able to use. One of the most useful for the United Kingdom is the rateable value of property, and this was used by Clark and Jones (1971)[3] in their study of demand for housing. Holm (1967)[4] has tried a solution which selects a few characteristics. He classifies each dwelling 'according to its technical fittings and equipment and its date of construction', using an actual example of a medium-sized Swedish town. Thus although it is difficult to measure housing units, it is not unrealistic to attempt to do so.

PRICE OF HOUSING

The price of housing has in Fig. 4.1 been expressed in some arbitrary unit of money. It represents the amount out of his annual income which the individual is prepared to give up for housing. It may take the form of rent to a public authority or a private owner, of interest payable on borrowed capital to purchase a property or, if he has used his own capital, of the interest which he has forgone on his investments in order to transfer his capital to property ownership. This is the real rate of interest or the opportunity cost of the use of his capital in this way.

In the case of public authority housing the relevant price is that charged to the individual, i.e. after deduction of subsidies. Subsidiary costs of housing related directly to the amount consumed should be included, e.g. repair, maintenance and service charges on private-sector flats sold on a long lease, local authority rates (taxes), repair and maintenance of the dwelling. For houses purchased by the individual there are complications arising from the taxation position and from the effects of inflation and price changes in the value of assets. These are dealt with in some detail below.

Effect of Taxation

The effects of tax relief on house purchase can be very substantial. Income tax and the complex system of relief from taxation in operation in the United Kingdom means that the rate of interest which should be used to arrive at the real price of housing should be adjusted for income tax so that it is the rate which is actually paid after all tax allowances which should be considered or, in the case of purchase out of capital, the interest after all tax deductions which is the forgone interest.

Effect of Changes in the Value of Capital Assets

If the value of money is changing, e.g. with inflation, or if there is a change in the price of dwellings or other relevant assets, some adjustment ought to be made to the rate of interest considered as the price of housing.

Table 4.1 shows the factors which have to be considered for purchase of a house both out of borrowed capital and out of own capital. It is assumed in the case of borrowed capital that the loan is not available for use except on house purchase, i.e. that the increase in the value of the capital in an alternative use (d) is nil. Considering the borrowed capital situation first, the net rate of interest is the actual rate payable minus tax relief, i.e. $c = a - b = 5$ per cent in the example given. If the value of the dwelling increases, this has to be offset against the net rate of interest and the effective rate becomes $f=c-e=-5$ per cent.

If on the other hand the purchase is made out of the person's own capital, then the rate of interest in its alternative use has to be considered minus the tax payable, i.e. $i=g-h=5$ per cent. However, this capital was increasing its value too, so that the effective rate of interest which is forgone is $k=i+j=$ 10 per cent. Then the effective rate of interest for house purchase is the effective forgone rate minus the rate of increase in the value of the dwelling, i.e. $m=k-l=0$ per cent.

TABLE 4.1
Effective Rate of Interest as the Price of Housing

Borrowed capital	%	Own capital	%
a Rate of interest payable on loan	8	g Rate of interest in alternative use	8
b Tax relief	3	h Tax payable	3
c Rate of interest net of tax, i.e. $a-b$	5	i Rate of interest net of tax, i.e. $g-h$	5
d Increase in value of capital in alternative use	0	j Increase in value of capital in alternative use	5
		k Effective forgone rate of interest, i.e. $i+j$	10
e Increase in value of dwelling	10	l Increase in value of dwelling	10
f Effective rate of interest, i.e. $c-e$	−5	m Effective rate of interest, i.e. $k-l$	0

If this rate f for borrowed capital is used to calculate the price of housing in relation to other commodities, the price becomes negative, i.e. the individual is paid to consume housing units, and demand would be infinite; but this clearly does not conform to reality. The reasons are as follows:

(i) It is not possible to obtain credit to purchase a house unless income is fairly high, and then it is easy only for the first house.

(ii) There are other forms of capital investment besides housing which include some hedge against inflation, e.g. equities.

(iii) There are costs of consumption of housing other than rent, notably rates, maintenance and cleaning (see above).

(iv) House purchase is regarded as a long-term matter and few persons wish to move at frequent intervals. Although the effective rate of interest at the moment of purchase may be negative, it is a matter of uncertainty whether or not it will remain so, as there may be a change in interest rate, taxation rates or inflation.

(v) Most people do not calculate the cost of housing in terms of real costs but in terms of actual current outgoings. In the case of the adjustment of the rate of interest for taxation, the time period is relatively short. However, in the case of adjustment for inflation, the time period is extremely long – the period until the house is sold. Even when it is sold the family must live somewhere and will not normally wish to reduce its standard of housing. A similar house will cost a similar price and again the capital gain is not realised (unless the mortgage is increased). In other words, the payment to buy housing comes at the end of the period of consumption of housing, or with a reduction in the consumption of housing due, for example, to children leaving home.

For these reasons it is not very satisfactory to deal with the effects of price changes in the capital assets by making an adjustment to the interest rate payable. It is probably more appropriate to confine the price to the net rate of interest after tax and to consider the effect of price changes as a shift in the demand curve.

SHIFT IN THE DEMAND CURVE

The demand curve shows what amount of a good would be demanded at various prices. It applies to a particular point in time so that all variables other than price are constant. If there are changes in the circumstances of the individual over time, the demand curve will change in position or shape or both. This is known as a shift in the demand curve. A change in circumstances may be caused by any of an infinite number of causes, such as a change in income, a change in his taste for housing by reason of advertising for example, a change in his ownership of capital, etc. It is suggested too that there would be a shift in the demand curve of an individual if he came to anticipate a change in the value of housing for purchase (although only for those individuals considering house purchase).

A change in income is particularly important for housing demand because housing expenditure accounts for such a high proportion of total income. As income rises there would usually be a shift of the demand curve upwards to, say, D_2 in Fig. 4.1. The effects of income changes are analysed in depth in the Appendix.

Capital ownership will clearly have a considerable effect on the demand for housing, since it increases the resources available for the consumption of housing. A discussion of its treatment is also included in the Appendix. Clearly, however, any change in the ownership of capital by an individual would tend to shift his demand curve.

TOTAL DEMAND CURVE

So far the analysis has been confined to the nature of the individual's demand curve for housing. It is now possible to see how, using the individual demand curves, a curve showing the total demand for housing units can be derived. Suppose in Fig. 4.2 that (a), (b) and (c) represent the individual demand curves for housing of three persons. These three curves can be summed in (d) to see how much all three consumers together would demand at given prices. Thus at price 30 the demand would be 4·5 units from (a) plus 2 units from (b) plus 7·5 units from (c) to give a total of 14 units in (d).

Just as three can be summed so, in theory, can the demand curves of the total number of consumers and the total demand curve obtained, although of course changing the scale on a horizontal axis. The total demand curve will slope down to the right. It may well be convex to the origin since most individual demand curves are of this shape. However, in the total of individual curves there may be some which are not convex and these could be sufficient to make the total demand curve other than convex – perhaps approximating to a straight line.

It is clear in the derivation of individual demand curves from indifference curves and price (see Appendix) that they represent what the individual will actually require at various prices. Thus total demand curves, sometimes called economic or effective demand curves, show what the community is able and willing to pay for and should not be confused with need, which is discussed below.

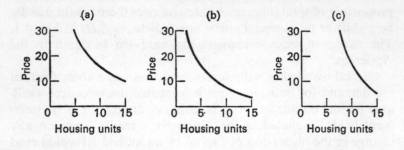

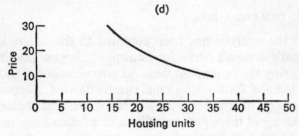

FIG. 4.2. Summation of individual demand curves

PRICE ELASTICITY OF DEMAND

In order to describe the demand curve more precisely, the concept of elasticity is useful. Elasticity of demand expresses the percentage change in the amount demanded in response to a percentage change in price. It is perhaps most easily understood in terms of the total amount spent on a commodity. If, with a fall in price, the amount demanded increases more than proportionately to the price change, so that the total amount the consumer spends on a commodity rises, then the demand is said to be elastic, i.e. it stretches (hence elastic) much in response to price. If, however, with a fall in price the amount demanded increases less than proportionately to the price fall, so that the total amount the consumer spends on a commodity falls, then the demand is said to be inelastic. The neutral position arises where the amount the consumer spends is the same whatever the price. In this situation demand is neither elastic nor inelastic and, as will be seen below, when the measurement of elasticity is discussed, is expressed as elasticity 1 or $e=1$. Demand is likely to be elastic if there are close substitutes for the product (e.g. flats as opposed to houses) and inelastic if the commodity has no close substitutes (e.g. all housing).

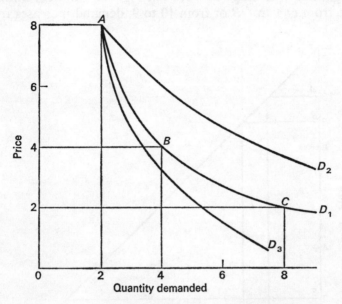

FIG. 4.3. Varying price elasticities of demand

The demand curve of $e=1$ is the shape shown in Fig. 4.3 as D_1. No matter what the price, the area of any rectangle drawn under the curve representing the amount spent, i.e. price multiplied by quantity demanded, is always constant. Thus in Fig. 4.3, at A, B and C and at all intermediate points the consumer will spend 16 money units on the product. This type of curve is described as a rectangular hyperbola.

When the curve is flatter than the curve $e=1$, then e is greater than 1 and the curve is elastic. When the curve is less flat than $e=1$, then e is less than 1, i.e. the curve is inelastic. In Fig. 4.3 the curve D_2 has e greater than 1 and the curve D_3 has e smaller than 1.

More precise numerical values may be put to elasticity. Price elasticity of demand for good x

$$= - \frac{\text{Percentage change in quantity of } x \text{ demanded}}{\text{Percentage change in the price of } x}$$

The minus sign is simply a convenience of definition to make elasticity positive. Let us consider this definition in terms of a straight line with slope $=-1$, as in Fig. 4.4. Consider a fall in price from OA to OB or from 10 to 9; demand increases from

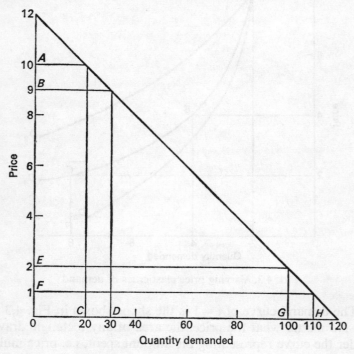

FIG. 4.4. Demand curve with slope $= -1$.

OC to OD or from 20 to 30, i.e. with a fall in price of 1 from 10 by 10 per cent, the quantity demanded increases by 50 per cent.

Therefore
$$e = - \frac{\dfrac{50}{100}}{\dfrac{-10}{100}} = - \frac{50}{-10} = 5.$$

At a different part of the curve, consider a fall in price from *OE* to *OF* or from 2 to 1. Then demand increases from *OG* to *OH* or 100 to 110. In this case

$$e = -\frac{\frac{10}{100}}{\frac{-50}{100}} = -\frac{10}{-50} = \frac{1}{5}.$$

It is clear from this illustration that a straight line, i.e. a curve of constant slope, has different elasticities over its length. This is because it is the change in relation to the total which is expressed by elasticity, not the change by itself.

INCOME ELASTICITY OF DEMAND

A parallel concept to price elasticity is income elasticity. Income elasticity expresses the percentage change in the amount demanded in response to a percentage change in income.

Thus, for example, if income increases by 20 per cent and the amount of a commodity purchased increases by 10 per cent, then income elasticity of demand is $\frac{1}{2}$; if the amount purchased increases by 20 per cent, it is 1, and if the amount increases by 40 per cent, then the income elasticity of demand is 2. In broad terms, if income elasticity of demand is less than 1 the commodity is a necessity, and if it is greater than 1 it is a luxury. As the proportion of income spent on housing is high, income elasticity of demand is an important concept for the consideration of the demand for housing. Several attempts have been made to measure it using either time-series analysis, in which the available data on housing demand are analysed in relation to income changes over a period of years, or cross-section analysis, in which housing demand is examined in relation to families living in various income groups in a given short period of time. The latter method has the advantage that the time period is too short for other conditions to have changed substantially.

ACTUAL ASSESSMENTS OF ELASTICITIES OF DEMAND

The early work on income elasticities of demand for housing was done in the United States, and Reid (1962)[5] drew on the work of Friedman (1957)[6] and others for her book *Housing and Income*, where she makes an exhaustive study of American data distingushing between 'normal' income and actual income. Normal income is the stable income which potential customers of housing 'have in mind when making decisions'.

In the last two years there has been a burst of activity in the United Kingdom in estimating income elasticities and price elasticities of demand for housing, probably on account of the change in the relationship of the number of households and the number of dwellings which makes some understanding of elasticities essential for forecasting.

Most of the work has concentrated on private-sector housing for owner occupation and refers to expenditure on housing as a whole, which would of course include the cost of land. Permanent income elasticity of demand based on cross-section analysis ranges from 0·6 to 1·0 (Holmans, 1970;[7] Clark and Jones, 1971;[3] Johnston *et al.*, 1972;[8] Vipond and Walker 1972[9]), largely depending on the consideration given to age of head of household, social class, etc. Time-series analysis tends to show higher elasticities (Whitehead, 1971[10]), probably due to changes in the underlying conditions in the market for housing and in the population structure.

Holmans, Whitehead, and Clark and Jones have also worked on price elasticity and find values ranging from 0·26 to 0·6. The price elasticity of demand for the dwelling (excluding land) is likely to be considerably less elastic than for housing as a whole by reason of the high proportion of the cost of land.

For the public sector the elasticity of demand for housing by the individuals who are to occupy the dwellings has had relatively little relevance. However, it is important for the building industry that it should have some idea of price elasticity of demand of local authorities as clients for new building. It seems that overall, since the assessment of their demand is made on need and since, as in private housing, the price of land is a large component of cost, the price elasticity of demand for the dwelling is likely to be rather inelastic.

It should be noted that in a situation of cost limits, i.e. where the price of a dwelling is fixed, if price changes, the amount demanded in terms of standards or units of housing (not dwelling units) falls, so that the price elasticity of housing becomes 1.

DEMAND FOR NEW HOUSING*

The analysis so far has been concerned with the demand for housing, irrespective of whether the housing is stock or newly constructed. The demand for new housing will depend on the demand for all housing, the stock of housing and the amount of replacement; while the amount actually built will depend on this demand and the building industry's supply curve.

In Fig. 4.5A are the demand and supply curves for all housing, and in Fig. 4.5B the demand curve for new housing and the supply curve for new housing both expressed as demand and supply per annum. All curves in these diagrams have been drawn for convenience and ease of exposition as straight lines.

Suppose that at a certain date, say 1 January in year 1, the demand for all housing is shown in Fig. 4.5A by the curve D_1 and the stock by S_1 at 120 million notional housing units. Price is P_1, which balances supply and demand.

Assume that the housing supply industry is in a state of equilibrium and at price P_1 is prepared to build nothing for stock, as is shown by its supply curve for new housing hs. In such an equilibrium position it might still at that price build for replacement, in which case the supply curve hs would shift to the right, but this is not shown in the diagram and in this analysis for the sake of simplification replacement is ignored.

The supply curve of the housing industry is conceived as including the supply curves of private housing developers, local and other public authorities acting as developers, whether letting or selling at a subsidised price or not. Since it is housing accommodation which is being supplied, the price must include an allowance for the cost of land as well as for the actual costs of construction, all expressed as an annual rate in a manner similar to that used for the analysis of demand. In view therefore of the high costs of land in many areas, the housing supply

*An analysis of the effect of rent control similar to that presented in this section is undertaken by Lindbeck (1967).[11]

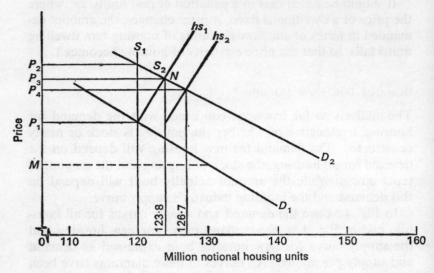

FIG. 4.5A. Demand and supply of all housing

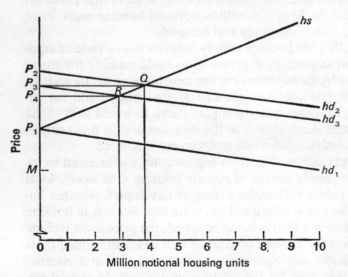

FIG. 4.5B. Demand and supply of new housing (annual)

curve will be determined to a relatively small extent by the actual costs of construction.

The demand curve for new housing at 1 January in year 1 may be derived from D_1 in Fig. 4.5A. From D_1 the demand for new housing at price P_1 is nil since the existing stock meets demand, while at price M it is 130 million units minus the stock of 120 million or 10 million units. This is shown in the annual demand curve for new housing hd_1 in Fig. 4.5B.

Assume that for some exterior reason, such as immigration or a rise in incomes, the demand D_1 shifts to D_2 on 1 January of year 2. As at a certain day the stock cannot be increased, the stock remains the same at S_1 and the new price becomes P_2.

Just as the annual demand curve for new housing hd_1 in Fig. 4.5B was derived from D_1 in Fig. 4.5A, so the housing industry's supply curve for all housing can be derived from the annual supply curve hs in Fig. 4.5B, adding it on to the stock. Thus the supply curve for all housing during year 2 will be hs_1 in Fig. 4.5A. The new point of equilibrium at the end of year 2 will be at N with a stock of 123·8 million notional housing units and a price P_3. For year 3 the analysis is repeated with the supply curve becoming hs_2, the new stock 126·7 and the new price P_4. This process continues until a new long-term equilibrium is established. Whether this is at a price above or below the price P_1 depends on the shape of the curves, for example whether there are any factors pushing up the long-run supply curve. It is clear that any shift in the demand curve will take some years to work its way through the system because the net annual additions to stock are very small in relation to the total stock of housing.

Fig. 4.5B shows the same situation viewed from the housing supply industry position. It was already seen that with the initial demand D_1 in Fig. 4.5A in equilibrium, there was no building for stock and the price was P_1. When the demand curve for all housing shifts to D_2 in Fig. 4.5A there is a new derived annual demand curve for new housing of hd_2 in Fig. 4.5B. This cuts the annual supply curve hs at Q with price P_3 and output of the industry 3·8 million units.

In year 3 the industry is faced with another demand curve hd_3, for at price P_3 the demand for addition to stock is now nil (at N in Fig. 4.5A, D_2 and S_2 cut) and the annual demand curve becomes hd_3 in Fig. 4.5B, which cuts hs at R with an output of 2·9 million units and a price P_4. Thus the housing supply industry jumps from meeting only replacement demand (not shown in the diagram) in year 1 to an output of replacement demand plus 3·8 million units for stock in year 2, plus 2·9 million in year 3 and decreasing in subsequent years until a new equilibrium is established. The large fluctuations in demands on the industry which arise from an increase in demand for the services provided by a capital good are discussed in greater detail in Chapter 5.

MANY DIFFERENT HOUSING MARKETS

At several stages in the foregoing analysis reference was made to the different types of housing demand and supply, notably housing to buy and housing to rent, housing provided by the private sector and that by the public sector, sometimes at a subsidised price. In practice there are separate and overlapping markets for a large range of types of housing, including flats, houses, bungalows; houses in various localities; as well as the more obvious rent/buy markets and the private-sector/public-sector choice. To consider the whole housing market as one is a simplification which must be dropped as the analysis is used to understand specific situations. Analysis below of the private-sector demand and supply position for housing to rent and housing to purchase provides a framework within which other specialised demand and supply situations may be examined.

HOUSING TO RENT AND HOUSING TO PURCHASE IN THE PRIVATE SECTOR

The demand for housing to purchase and housing to rent is complex because the individual is likely to have a definite preference either for rented or for purchased accommodation, but will, if he has the financial resources, be prepared to switch from one to the other if the price of one becomes too high or if the supply is not available.

Consider the situation in Fig. 4.6. RD_1 is the demand curve for housing units to rent made up of the individual demand curves whose first choice is to rent rather than buy. Curve PD_1

is the demand curve for all other persons, i.e. those whose first choice is to buy. *RS* is the stock of dwellings for renting, *PS* is the stock of dwellings for ownership.

In the rented sector the market price for rented dwellings

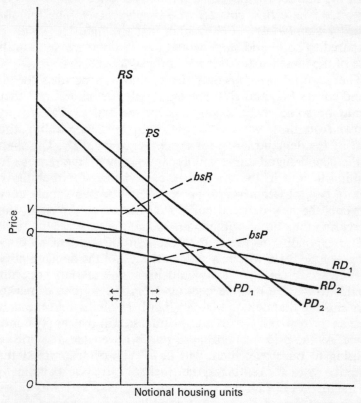

FIG. 4.6. Housing to rent and housing to purchase in the private sector

would be *OQ*, i.e. the price at which supply curve *RS* (=stock) cuts the demand curve *RD*₁.

In conditions such as those existing in the United Kingdom, where there is partial rent control and uncertainty as to the future extent of rent control, the housing industry (including developers) is unlikely to be confident in the long-run rate of return from housing to rent and will therefore be prepared to supply only at a rather high price, i.e. the building supply curve for rent is *bsR*. This lies above the demand curve and therefore no building will take place. For the same reason there is unlikely to be appreciable net movement of housing from the stock for sale to the stock for rent.

In the market for purchase the market price would be *OV*, the price where *PD*$_1$ cuts *PS* (the supply curve). The building industry supply curve *bsP* is such that the industry would be prepared to build and stock would eventually increase as in the case of the increase of the stock in Fig. 4.5A–B.

There would not, however, be equilibrium because the demand curves *PD*$_1$ and *RD*$_1$ represent only first choice and there would be some reallocation once prices and availability are known from those wishing to rent to those wishing to buy, thus shifting the demand curve for purchase to, say, *PD*$_2$. The shape of the new demand curve will depend partly on the reasons for wishing to rent in the first place, e.g. whether for mobility or lack of capital (security) or income. The building supply curve *bsP* cuts the new demand curve *PD*$_2$ further to the right, thus increasing the output of the industry and the stock.

Corresponding to the shift to the right of the demand curve for purchase there will be a shift to the left of the demand curve to rent, to, say, *RD*$_2$. This would lower the market price and would attract back some persons from the purchase market, thus shifting that demand curve slightly to the left. At the same time as the demand curves are shifting, so will the supply curves move. As the price of housing to rent is lower than the price of housing to purchase, there will be a shift of accommodation from the stock for renting to the stock for purchase as indicated by the arrows in Fig. 4.6. There will thus be a series of adjustments of decreasing size until equilibrium is achieved. These adjustments will be of three types, namely:

(*a*) changes in the choices of the consumers for accommodation to rent and accommodation to purchase;

(*b*) changes in the stock of accommodation to rent and to purchase as a result of a movement from one to the other;

(*c*) changes in the stock of accommodation as a result of new building.

The situation is complicated by rent control and the effect of this has been analysed, notably by Lindbeck (1967)[11] and Stahl

(1967).[12] Stahl includes in his analysis a consideration of the effect of rent control on consumer satisfaction. In general terms, if there is rent control the price would be lower than the market price but the supply would be the same, implying some non-price rationing or queueing system. The system adopted would partly determine the shape of the demand curves in the process of adjustment, leading towards an equilibrium situation as outlined above.

FORECASTING THE DEMAND FOR NEW HOUSING

Although the theoretical analysis provides a background of fundamental understanding of the housing market, in practice only parts of it can yet be used as the basis of forecasting. There are broadly three methods of forecasting, all using aggregated data :

(a) to build up the total 'needs' for new housing and then to decide over what period need will be satisfied;

(b) to consider directly the factors which affect economic demand and forecast these to arrive at total housing demand;

(c) to look at past trends in housebuilding and in the factors which affected it and project these forward.

In practice, almost all forecasts of housing demand are a fusion of these three methods. Holmans (1971)[7] forecasts in some detail the demand for various types of accommodation in terms of the people who are likely to demand a given type and of the other types of accommodation from which they will be moving. He makes use of economic demand methods as well as taking into account the long-term factors. His is the most direct application of the theoretical analysis of adjustments between various markets.

Need-based Forecasts

The first method, i.e. method (a), uses assessment of 'need' for all sectors of housing together. Need is defined as the difference between an accepted standard of housing provision and the extent to which the stock reaches this standard. It is dependent on requirements for net new household formation; requirements to replace dwellings cleared in slum-clearance schemes and for other purposes such as road building; and requirements to increase the stock in relation to existing households to provide a margin of vacant dwellings for mobility. In addition, it is usually recognised that not all existing dwellings will be available to provide first homes as some will be used for second homes. This need assessment assumes that certain standards of housing provision are to be achieved. These standards are often laid down by government and therefore can change suddenly, but the underlying basis for them is usually public opinion or the social conscience, which tends slowly to raise its conception of what is an acceptable minimum as the standard of living rises.

The future number of households will, apart from immigration and emigration, be affected by the population and its age structure. Both these are known in so far as they affect the number of households, say, up to fifteen years ahead, because all heads of households are now born. Death rates are relatively constant. On the assumption that the same number of persons in any age group will head households (the headship rate) as at present, the total number of households can be predicted with reasonable accuracy.

This last assumption is, however, a very doubtful one. Firstly, the marriage rate may change; secondly, there is a tendency for more young, single people to leave the family unit and establish separate households; and thirdly, at the other extreme of the age range, widows and widowers are more prepared to live separately rather than live with the younger generation. In Scandinavia particularly, headship rates among young people have risen very rapidly in the post-war years (United Nations, 1963),[13] and are now substantially above those in the United Kingdom. Some definite forecast must therefore be made of headship rates.

In conceptual terms an increase in the number of households will add to the number of individual demand curves which have to be summed to arrive at the total demand curve. It will also shift the individual demand curves because of the different requirements in space and amenity of the traditional household with children living in and of the new smaller households. Although one would not expect the total demand curve for housing units to go up in proportion to the number of households because the households are small, it would be expected to rise substantially because of the relatively high minimum requirement of a separate household. The space and amenities required per person are generally greater for a small household than for a large one.

Once the standard has been set, information on the existing dwellings is required to determine how much of the stock needs replacement. Census data on the condition of the housing stock are available at regular intervals. The major problem with this and to a lesser extent other aspects of the need forecast is to determine over what period of years needs can be met. For this purpose, recourse is usually had to method (*c*), i.e. to a consideration of what the actual rate of construction could be in the foreseeable future.

The number of houses which should be replaced each year will in most cases be greater than would be demanded at the ruling price by the occupants of the slums, either because they do not have a high degree of satisfaction at the prospect of moving to a better house or because they have too low an income. The slum-clearance programme is higher than that which would be achieved by the economic demand of individuals, and therefore social policy has to be translated into economic demand by some sort of public subsidy. Similarly, the vacancies desired for mobility may be more or less than would ultimately be provided by economic forces. Second homes by contrast are entirely a matter of demand (of individuals or firms) and not of need.

Forecasts of Economic Demand

The forecast of economic demand (category (*b*)) refers mostly to the private sector. Clark and Jones (1971)[3] made such a forecast, first making estimates of income elasticity and price elasticity of demand for housing and then applying these to their own forecast incomes derived from the expected rise in consumer expenditure per head and in population. They also made various assumptions about the real cost of housing. It is expected that the use of the results of the recent researches into elasticities will produce many more forecasts of this type in the future.

The forecast of incomes to which to apply the elasticity of demand is in itself difficult, for, because of the underlying individual nature of demand, it is not sufficient simply to forecast the growth in personal disposable incomes. The distribution of these incomes is very significant and hence forecasts should be made, *inter alia*, of the level of unemployment and the relative rates of increase in wages and salaries and other types of income.

The supply of credit or savings must also be taken into account in forecasting economic demand. So far as the demand curve of the individual is concerned, if capital is expressed as income equivalent, no adjustment is required for credit, as credit is simply the capital which the income can command. So long as the rate of interest is holding the balance between the demand and supply of credit, no further theoretical adjustment is necessary. An increase in the supply of credit or savings, i.e. capital, means a shift in the demand curve.

In order to predict in aggregated terms whether this shift will take place and by how much, changes in savings by private individuals are important and also the supply of credit – in the United Kingdom particularly that supplied by building societies. In recent years there have been long periods when the loans made by building societies have been restricted by the inflow of funds to them and the demand for credit was not therefore being met at the ruling rate of interest. This means that the effective demand for housing was not represented by the total demand curve built up by summing individuals' demand curves on the method outlined, but was shifted downwards by the overall credit shortage. Changes in the rate of interest alter the price of housing in so far as this is represented by annual outgoings on house purchase.

Extension of Past Trends

This last method of forecasting is most useful when it is a reasonable assumption that there are no great changes in the underlying factors determining demand and supply for housing or when the period is so long that fluctuations around a trend are unimportant.

Attention is then concentrated on the changes which can reasonably be foreseen in the components of housing demand,

and the trend is adjusted as necessary. The factors which are considered in such forecasts are similar to those used under methods (*a*) and (*b*) but particularly those in (*b*), i.e. incomes, supply of credit or savings, the rate of interest, house prices, etc.

5 Demand for Industrial and Commercial Building

The demand for factories and offices is not dependent directly on the ultimate consumer but on the producers of goods for the ultimate consumer. It is known as derived demand. Its analysis benefits from the concern of economists with the relationships between investment and consumption. The initial discussion will be mainly in terms of industrial building followed by a consideration of the extent to which the same analysis is applicable to commercial building.

ACCELERATION PRINCIPLE

The acceleration principle states that if the demand for any consumption good increases, the demand for the investment goods used in its production will increase at a greater rate. This may be illustrated by a numerical example, as shown in Table 5.1.

TABLE 5.1

Illustration of the Acceleration Principle

Year	Demand for good A during year	Demand for stock of buildings to produce A during year	Demand for new buildings to produce A to be built in preceding year		
			Replacement [a]	Net increase	Total
1	100	200	10	0	10
2	100	200	10	0	10
3	100	200	10	40	50
4	120	240	12	20	32
5	130	260	13	0	13
6	130	260	13	−20	0
7	120	240	12	0	5
8	120	240	12	0	12
9	120	240	12	0	12

[a]Assuming replacement equal to 5 per cent of stock per annum.

In year 1, year 2 and year 3 the demand for good A is constant at 100 and the stock of buildings to produce A is also constant at 200. Five per cent of the buildings are replaced each year so that the demand from this source is constant at 10. Then in year 4 the demand for good A rises by 20 per cent to 120, and the demand for the stock of buildings rises to 240. Provided that the rise was anticipated, the new buildings to produce this output in year 4 should have been built in year 3. Thus in years 1 and 2 there is no demand for net increase in buildings. In year 3 there is a demand of 40 to enable production to be increased in year 4. In year 5 the demand for good A continues to rise, but at a decreasing rate, to 130. The demand for the stock of buildings rises to 260, showing a shortfall of 20 which must be constructed in year 4. Note that the demand for good A is still rising but the demand for new buildings is falling because it is related to the rate of increase in total demand which is already falling. By year 6 there is no longer any expansion in demand for good A and the demand for new building in year 5 falls to the replacement level of 13. If in year 7 the demand for good A decreases by 10, then the stock requirements will decrease by 20 and there will not even be a replacement demand in year 6 because 13 units of the surplus stock of buildings will be used for replacement. In year 7 there will still be 7 units of surplus capacity to set against the replacement need of 12, so that new building will be only 5 units. Not until year 8 will there be a real replacement need of 5 per cent of the stock of buildings.

The acceleration principle operates because investment goods including buildings have a long life so that the stock constitutes a very important element in the total situation. If the life of buildings were the the same as the production period under consideration – a year in this case – the demand for buildings would increase at the same rate as output but a year in advance.

The acceleration principle therefore applies to all investment in buildings and is clear from the housing analysis where, the stock of buildings being high, the new demand for buildings is very dependent on the increase in demand for housing. The only reasons why traditionally the acceleration principle is used to help explain the demand for industrial buildings rather than housing are that (*a*) changes in demand of most manufactured goods for ultimate consumption are more obvious than changes in the demand for housing, and (*b*) the housing demand is so dependent on other determinants such as government social policy which may mask the effects of the accelerator.

PRACTICAL MODIFICATIONS IN APPLICATION OF THE ACCELERATION PRINCIPLE

In fact, although there are fluctuations in the demand for industrial building, they are not as large as they would be on the basis of the acceleration principle alone. Some of the reasons are as follows:

(*a*) There is often some surplus capacity in industry and it is therefore possible to increase output by increasing employment by overtime, shift working, etc.

(*b*) An industrial building is only a casing for the manufacturing process. The layout of machinery within a building can often be completely altered and modernised without altering the building itself. Even if the building is altered, this would probably appear in the statistics as repair and maintenance rather than new industrial building.

(*c*) If the increase in demand in manufacturing industry is not accompanied by expectations that the demand will continue, then output will be increased by other methods even though in the long run they might be more expensive. Thus, in Table 5.1, if the entrepreneur had anticipated that the increase in demand in years 5 and 6 would be temporary only, he would not have increased his stock of buildings.

(*d*) The willingness of entrepreneurs to increase their capacity will depend, in addition to expectations of demand, on profits and expectations of profit. Thus if demand is rising and costs are expected to rise too, then expectations of profits may be such that entrepreneurs will not expand. Similarly, their ability and willingness to expand will depend on other factors such as the availability of capital and the cost of capital.

(*e*) Ability to expand may be affected by government policy not only in the price and availability of credit but also by physical controls on development, for example through Industrial Development Certificates.

(*f*) Technological change may induce requirements for new buildings for replacement: for example, improved atmospheric conditions required in cotton manufacture may need new factory buildings and computers require a fully controlled atmosphere. The rate of technological change and hence of the increase in demand will fluctuate over time.

RESPONSE OF DEMAND TO PRICE

It is important for the construction industry to have some idea of the elasticity of demand for industrial buildings. Because the demand is derived, it is dependent on many more things than price. For example, an industrialist who is considering whether or not to increase his productive capacity by putting up a new factory must consider the overall profitability of the capital invested and will probably not be willing to undertake the project unless he has an expectation of, say, 15–20 per cent return on capital for a minimum of twenty years. The capital invested will be, say 20 per cent buildings and 80 per cent plant and machinery[1], and if he wishes to undertake the project he must have both together. Consequently a rise in the price of building by 10 per cent will be a rise in the cost of the project by 2 per cent. This is very small in relation to the margin of error in the calculation of the 15–20 per cent. Moreover, the capital costs will in many cases be a relatively small part of total costs. Hence the demand curve for industrial buildings is likely to be relatively inelastic.

FORECASTS OF THE LEVEL OF INDUSTRIAL BUILDING

Because of the close relationship between the level of industrial investment, the level of industrial production and hence the health of the economy, it would be expected that forecasts of the level of industrial building could be made on the basis of certain assumptions on the level of industrial production and gross domestic product. Various attempts have been made to use econometric methods to obtain long-term forecasts, notably recently by the Joint Working Party on Demand and Output

Forecasts of the E.D.C.s for Building and Civil Engineering (1971).[2]

The most obvious relationship is that given by the incremental capital–output ratios (ICORs). This is the relation between net capital formation in any period and the increase in output during that period. In the example of Table 5.1 above, because the output has been lagged a year after investment the ICOR has an odd value of 40/0 or ∞ in year 3. Had the output not been lagged, the ICOR in year 4 would have been 40/20 or 2 and in year 5 20/10 or 2. In all other years except year 7, when it would be negative, the ICOR would be nil. Various adjustments may be made to this crude ICOR, for example to exclude changes in output attributable to employment rather than to capital. The method depends on a reliable forecast of output, and once a figure for investment has been obtained this still has to be apportioned between plant and equipment and buildings and works.

Because of the apparently closer relationship of investment in plant and machinery than investment generally to output of manufacturing industry, attempts have been made first to forecast investment in plant and then to relate this to the output of buildings. This is essentially using the same relationships but undertaking the analysis in a different order and with perhaps a more logical sequence.

Other methods which depend less on forecasts of exogenous variables include relating investment in factory buildings directly to lagged gross domestic product and to profits, also suitably adjusted for the time trend.

None of these various methods has been found to give results which, when applied to periods in the past for which the outcome is known, inspire confidence in their use as the only method of forecasting. In the last resort, forecasters have to make a judgement of the likely level of output based partly on the results of this type of econometric analysis and partly on other indicators such as the level of Industrial Development Certificates.

COMMERCIAL BUILDING

By commercial building is meant the whole range of buildings other than industrial buildings for an enterprise engaged in the buying or selling of a product or service. It thus includes offices, hotels, garages, shops, etc., i.e. nearly all private building except for housing, industrial building and a few miscellaneous categories such as churches.

There is on the face of it no reason why the investment in these buildings should not be related to output, growth, profits, etc., in similar way to that for industrial building. The basic characteristic of long life in relation to the services or goods it helps to produce is present and so is a relationship to productive capacity.

This area could therefore be subjected to the same kind of research for econometric relationships as industrial building. The problem is that some of the difficulties mentioned for the application of the acceleration principle to industrial building apply even more to commercial building and, in addition, there are others:

(*a*) Commercial building is a more heterogeneous collection of buildings and therefore different equations for each type of building would need to be established. Data are not available in sufficient detail to enable this to be done. Moreover, as the types of building are more distinct (compared with the totality of industrial building), it becomes less relevant to consider their relationship to general factors such as output. The individual variations would not be expected to cancel each other out. More specific factors likely to affect types of commercial building include changes in tastes for entertainment, and technological change, e.g., automatic garaging.

(*b*) The capacity of an office and of some other types of building is less rigid than that of factories. It is usually possible in the short run to squeeze in extra personnel and equipment by lowering space standards.

(*c*) The importance of expectations of output and of profits, and of the availability and cost of financing capital, are as important for commercial building as for industrial building, but the users of commercial buildings and the financiers of them are often different people, thus complicating the demand factors.

(*d*) The state of the economy and of government policy is similarly important: for example, Office Development Permits affect office building. The Development of Tourism Act, 1969, has stimulated hotel building with loans and grants.

(*e*) The commercial sector is probably more concerned to present a good public image than the industrial sector and may be dependent on this for its profits, e.g. in retailing.

As in the case of industrial building, the elasticity of demand for commercial building is likely to be low. However, because of (*b*) above it may be rather more elastic than that of industrial building.

Forecasts of commercial building are usually based on a qualitative analysis of the underlying factors affecting the various sectors, sometimes supported by econometric work along the lines of that mentioned above under industrial building.

OTHER DERIVED DEMAND

Although the clear cases of derived demand are industrial and commercial building in the private sector, some of the public-sector demand is substantially derived demand. Clear examples are the nationalised electricity and gas industries and, of course, steel. Others, such as transport and water supply, are partly derived demand and partly determined by social policy.

6 Demand for Social-type Construction

The two preceding chapters on demand for construction started by considering the factors which were relevant to the decision to build in a broad sector of demand and the theoretical concepts which were of assistance in understanding the interrelationships of the relevant factors. This chapter deals with a heterogeneous sector of construction in which the common features are that the product is used by a large number of persons or households collectively, e.g. hospitals, museums, roads, schools, or that it is used by persons or households individually but who individually are neither able nor willing to pay for the product and which the 'community' decides should be available.

Housing in the public authority sector comes partly into this category, although it is also dealt with in Chapter 4 on demand for buildings for the direct enjoyment of individuals. In that chapter the supply curve of the housing supply industry was taken as given and consideration was focused on the demand side. The supply curve for housing in the public sector is, however, determined by the same sort of considerations as those affecting other types of social demand and hence public authority housing is included in this chapter.

DIFFICULTIES OF A THEORETICAL APPROACH

There is unfortunately at the moment no body of economic theory which significantly adds to our understanding of the determination of construction demand for social-type projects. Welfare economics can make substantial contributions to decision-making on many matters of public expenditure, but on choices between comparatively small areas of expenditure all widely different in kind it has little to offer. One reason for this is the lack of any basis for making interpersonal comparisons of satisfaction, so that the indifference curves of individuals between various types of construction expenditure cannot be summed. One is inevitably led to a sort of 'superman' (Little, 1957)[1] deciding what is good for the community, and a theory based on the opinion of one individual is hardly better than no theory at all.

Cost–benefit analysis is a technique which enables some of welfare economics to be applied in a practical situation. It rests on one of the basic theses of welfare economics that, if the sum of the value of the benefits of a course of action is greater than the sum of the costs of that action, then it would be possible in theory for those who receive the benefits to give compensation to the losers and still be better off. In this practical application there are great difficulties in assessing the value of advantages and disadvantages of a particular course of action. Thus its principal use tends to be in the comparison of the relative net benefits of similar alternative courses of action. Hence, where the errors in the method of assessment of costs and benefits occur to roughly the same degree in each alternative under consideration, their absolute magnitude is less important. Thus it is feasible to compare sites for an airport because the *types* of advantages and disadvantages are likely to be the same. However, the technique has much less validity when comparing, say, investment in hospitals with investment in airports, because one is concerned with, for example, putting a value on life and on health and comparing this with the value of greater business facilities and holidays. Clearly, the margin of error or disagreement in the assignment of such values is so great that it may well swamp the differences between the final assessment of net benefits or losses.

Prest and Turvey (1965)[2] come to a similar conclusion when they say that:

> The technique is more useful in the public utility area than in the social services area of government. Comparisons between, say, different road projects are more helpful than those between, say, road and water projects; and both these are likely to be more helpful than application in the fields of education, health, research and so on.

Output budgeting or a planning and programming budgeting system (P.P.B.), as it is termed in the United States and Canada, suffers from the same drawbacks for our present purposes as cost–benefit analysis without having the advantages of its broad coverage.

FORECASTING IN PRACTICE

Notwithstanding the lack of theoretical help, it is important for the industry to be able to make some assessment of the social-type demands likely to be put to it. Indeed, this sector, excluding public authority housing, accounts for around a quarter of the demands on the construction industry and for most of the demands on that part of the industry specialising in civil engineering.

Of the three basic methods of forecasting outlined in Chapter 4, the most relevant to this sector are an assessment of needs together with a consideration of the resources likely to be available.

ASSESSMENTS OF STANDARDS

Standards of provision of services are not clearly defined, although some implicit standards usually exist and can be taken as a foundation on which to build. The very discussion of what minimum standards ought to be is helpful in policy-making. In housing there are two levels of standards: the level below which no dwelling ought to be occupied, i.e. slums; and the standard below which no new building should ideally be constructed – Parker-Morris. Between these two levels is an enormous range of conditions, and the lower-level standard may at any time be raised to include another chunk of housing. In studying demand, however, so long as the lowest level of standard is not achievable at any practicable rate of construction for many years, it is not necessary to consider the area in between the two standards in great detail because it is unlikely substantially to affect current policy.

The same applies to other areas of demand. If the lowest possible minimum standard is clearly not being achieved, then to argue at length on the acceptable minimum standard above this lowest minimum level will often be quite irrelevant for policy formation. Thus in the case of river pollution it is not fruitful for demand assessment to discuss the standards which should be established in new legislation, when the first priority, and one which would occupy the authorities for a number of years, is to attain the lower standards set by existing legislation. The first step therefore is to assess the lowest minimum standard and see in broad terms how nearly it is reached. Only if it is approached by present provision is it necessary to study in detail the changes taking place in policy and opinion which will establish a new standard.

SIZE, AGE AND CONDITION OF THE STOCK

Once some assessment of a standard has been made, it should be possible to assess the present stock and consider how far it falls short of the established standard. Whereas the standard itself is a matter of opinion and may therefore be difficult to assess, the stock is a matter of fact and is not basically difficult to establish, although the resources required may be substantial. For most of the public socially determined sectors very few data are available, with the possible exception of housing, schools and roads. Without these data any study of demand becomes very dubious. However, if the information can be obtained, some assessment of present need can be made.

FUTURE INCREASES IN NEED

Once present need is established a further step must be taken, namely the assessment of how far this need is likely to increase in the future, either because of changed standards already discussed, or changed populations to which these standards apply. Thus if the population of households increases, the number of dwelling units required will increase. If water provision is partly related to industrial output and industrial output increases, the consumption of water will increase.

TIME PERIOD OVER WHICH NEED LIKELY TO BE PROVIDED

Having established present and future need, it is still necessary to determine at what rate this backlog can be diminished. In the case of housing the wide variations in total demand assessments (ranging from 250,000 to 650,000 dwellings per annum) are principally accounted for by the different assumptions on the rate at which need will be transformed into effective demand. This is an area in which political decisions and priorities play a great part. However, the problem can often be narrowed by consideration of the constraints in transferring need into effective demand.

CONSTRAINTS

The first constraint (if it can be called this) is that in the bargaining process which goes on between protagonists of various sectors; once a sector has achieved a high rate of growth for a number of years it may well become the 'turn' of another sector. For similar reasons (as well as those discussed before) it is probably difficult for any sector to grow at an extremely high rate unless there is a great pressure of public opinion in its favour – as there may be, for example, for measures against pollution.

Apart from the political difficulty of a sector growing rapidly, there are practical difficulties. In the case of slum clearance, for example, to increase the rate of replacement in, say, five years' time may require action now on demolition orders, rehousing, clearing of sites, etc., and there may well be administrative and managerial bottlenecks even if there are no financial problems. To increase the rate of slum replacement in one year (assuming these preparatory processes have not been undertaken) may be virtually impossible. In the case of roads, 'generally about five years elapse from the time the Ministry decide to go ahead with a major project to the time when they are ready to invite tenders'.[3] The route for the M4 was not finally fixed until seven and a half years after the consulting engineers were appointed to report on possible routes (Brown, 1972).[4] This is because of planning and design problems and the time which has to be allowed for consideration of public objections.

Similar administrative, managerial and legal difficulties exist in many other sectors and, in addition, there may be bottlenecks in design, provision of finance and other stages in the process.

Lastly, if the rate of increase in this socially determined sector corresponds to a rapid rate of increase in other sectors, there could be inadequate capacity in the construction industry itself or in some of the materials industries. In 1964 the construction industry was stretched to capacity and there have been shortages of materials from time to time such as plasterboard, bricks, copper pipes and even manhole covers.

RESPONSE OF DEMAND TO PRICE

In normal circumstances the system of cost limits which operates in large parts of the public sector means that the overall cost of a unit of output is fixed, i.e. if in school building, for example, the cost of building a place rises by 1 per cent, then to keep within the cost limits, standards would need to fall by 1 per cent. In this case the elasticity of demand is 1.

In periods such as the early 1970s in the United Kingdom, in which the cost of building rose very steeply even after adjustment for the rate of inflation, the cost limits are raised but not necessarily by the amount of the increase in prices. In these circumstances demand is relatively inelastic.

In the case of individual projects demand may be very inelastic. A specific example which immediately comes to mind is the Sydney Opera House, where costs have gone up, there has been a great increase in its total cost, but the work done has altered little. There must be a number of other large projects where, partly because of the high real costs of abandoning work part of the way through a project, the costs have increased but have caused no diminution in the amount of building produced, i.e. there is a very low elasticity of demand.

For control of the public-sector expenditure as a whole, programmes are generally fixed at constant prices. This means that, if there is a general inflation, then the overall budget will normally be allowed to rise although usually with a time-lag causing expenditure to drag behind the rate of inflation, and in addition there may be cuts in the programme. Since elasticity of demand is usually expressed at constant prices, the normal elasticity concept is not appropriate here. However, an 'inflationary elasticity of demand' would be less than 1 in these circumstances.

7 How Demand is Put to the Industry

In order to appreciate the reaction of the industry to the demands upon it, it is necessary to understand the way in which the demand is placed. In this chapter a brief description of the process will be given with emphasis on those aspects which affect the type of theoretical analysis required to understand the behaviour of construction firms.

CLIENTS

The initiators of the whole construction process are the clients of the industry. In 1971, 56 per cent of the gross fixed-capital formation in construction was for government or semi-government bodies.[1] A small part of their contracting work is undertaken by their own labour force, but nevertheless government accounts directly or indirectly for over 50 per cent of all new work done by the industry.

The significance of the public sector as a client is great, for it implies that the principal clients of the industry have a continuing interest from the community point of view in the efficiency of the construction process and will often be commissioning large amounts of work. At the same time they are bound by the need to be impartial, and to be seen to be impartial, in commissioning work, for most of the organisations sponsoring the work are answerable directly or indirectly to the public for the way in which they spend their money. Because of the traditional method of accounting on a strictly annual basis, the public sector has difficulties in committing itself far ahead on work load (although every time it lets contracts extending over more than a year it is doing just this), particularly in areas of great political importance. A considerable amount of data on the behaviour of the public-sector client for school building is available in work undertaken by University College, London.[2]

Two types of private client must be considered, namely the client commissioning work for his own use, for example a company building a factory or an individual commissioning the design and construction of his own house, and the developer who is a client of the industry only because he wishes to sell or let the completed building. The latter type – the developer – may be further subdivided into those who are also builders and undertake the function of the main contractor themselves, and those who obtain the services of a contractor to undertake the work just as do non-developer clients.

No statistical data are available on the relative importance of these three categories. It is estimated, however, that the majority of private housing work is undertaken by developers for most of which the developer also functions as the main contractor, that a large part of private office building is for developers of whom only a small proportion are contractors, and a relatively small part of private industrial building is built by a contractor/developer. Overall the percentage of work in which the client and the main contractor are one firm is probably not more than 15 per cent of the total.

The determination of price for work undertaken by a developer is quite different from the price determination for construction work by a contractor, since it includes a consideration for land values, the price of capital, the system of taxation, etc. Hence it is excluded from the discussion of the way the contracting firm operates which is the subject of the remainder of this book.

On the private client and his behaviour relatively few data are available, although the unpublished study instigated by the National Economic Development Office[3] goes some way to filling gaps in knowledge. The survey was commissioned into the use made of the construction industry for new office or factory premises by commercial and industrial companies and the extent to which they were satisfied.

Most of the companies which participated in the survey had a turnover of under £10 million, and it is therefore not surprising that only a small percentage of their latest projects cost over £100,000.

It is interesting that about half the companies who had done some building had commissioned more than one building in the period 1 January 1968 to mid-1972 and 14 per cent had commissioned five or more. Thus a number of the private company clients are experienced.

The survey also finds that of the companies participating nearly half took a large part in the design process, about a third of the companies mainly costed the project themselves and over 10 per cent actually constructed the project with their own staff.

THE PROCESS: CLIENT TO CONTRACTOR

The process by which the work required goes from client to contractor is important in analysing the operation of the contracting industry and particularly the pricing mechanism. Once the client has decided to build, he will appoint some professional advisers. If the project is building, as opposed to civil engineering, he will usually first seek the help of an architect, although in some cases the quantity surveyor is appointed first. The architect may be assisted by independent consultants from other professions, e.g. structural engineers.

Instead of appointing an architect to advise him, the client may go to a company offering a complete service of design and construction, known as a package deal. In the N.E.D.O. survey[3] about a third of all factories built by the industry (as opposed to the firm's own labour) were by package deal, whereas the proportion for offices was about a quarter. Package deals are not confined to the private sector, for about 8 per cent of all local authority contracts for housing schemes in 1970 were package deals.[4] In the remainder of the public sector they are virtually unknown. The more usual procedure is to appoint a contractor to build after the design has been commissioned elsewhere.*

There are several methods of appointment of the main contractor. The traditional method is by inviting tenders to undertake the work based on the 'bill of quantities', i.e. the document listing all the items in the building drawn up by the quantity surveyor from the available plans and drawings. The contractor

*Bowley (1966)[5] is very critical of the system under which there is hardly any competition in design and in which design and construction are separated.

prices each item as well as putting in a figure for preliminaries which covers preparatory and general work. His final price will include his estimate for the cost to him of undertaking the project, a contribution to overheads and his profit.

In the case of open tendering the contract is advertised and any contractor may ask for the tender documents and put in his price for the job. In selective tendering, the client or his adviser makes a short-list of contractors whom he would like to undertake the work, and each of these is asked to put in a tender price. There are objections to open tendering, notably the lack of control of the client over the competence of the builder he is employing and waste of resources when many firms tender for the same job, for the prices for the contracts obtained must overall cover the cost of estimating on jobs not obtained. Although its use is decreasing, open tendering is still used, notably in the public sector. Research for the Phelps Brown Committee (1968)[6] found that it was used in about half of the contracts obtained by large firms* and about a third of those by small firms. *Action on the Banwell Report* (1967)[7] showed a steadily decreasing trend in open tendering in local authority housing and this has continued since,[4] so that whereas in the June quarter of 1964, 31 per cent of dwellings were built after open tender, in the year 1970 the figure was down to below 14 per cent. By 1965 only 13 per cent of the value of school-building contracts was by open tender. In the private-sector study on factories and offices,[3] open tendering was apparently considered so unimportant that it was not mentioned.

The public-sector work that used to be let by open tender is now largely let by some form of selective tender, either on the basis of approved lists or by a selection from contractors responding to invitations to seek selection.

On the other hand negotiation or a two-stage process involving first competition among a selected list and then negotiation have also grown and taken some of the share previously held by open tendering.

*In the Research Report, small firms are defined as those having fewer than 25 employees or between 25 and 79 employees with no operatives or 50 per cent or more operatives working on repair and maintenance or no contracts exceeding £20,000 in value. Large firms are all those which are not 'small'.

TABLE 7.1

Importance of Various Types of Tender: Main Contractor

	Private buildings		Local authority buildings		Local authority civil engineering			Central government	Nationalised industries	All work types, public and private	
	Factories (E) 1968-72	Offices a(E) 1968-72	Housing b 1970	Schools c 1965	Roads d 1965	Water d 1965	Sewerage d 1965	Civil Engineering d 1966	Civil Engineering d (E)	Large firms e (E)	Small firms e (E)
I. PERCENTAGE OF NUMBER OF CONTRACTS LET f											
Open tendering	0	0	25	26	58	33	48	n.a.	n.a.	48	47
Selective tendering (incl. invited list and select list)	35	38	54	59	37	55	40	n.a.	n.a.	26	19
Negotiation	29	36	13 ⎱	15 ⎱	4	12	11	n.a.	n.a.	22 ⎱	32 ⎱
Two-stage selective	9	6	⎰	⎰	1	0	1	n.a.	n.a.	⎰	⎰
Package deal	28	19	8	0	0	0	0	n.a.	n.a.	5	3
II. PERCENTAGE OF VALUE OF CONTRACTS LET f											
Open tendering	n.a.	n.a.	14	13	14	59	32	0	0	n.a.	n.a.
Selective tendering (incl. invited list and select list)	n.a.	n.a.	59	61	82	38	64	100	85	n.a.	n.a.
Negotiation	n.a.	n.a.	18 ⎱	26 ⎱	3	3	4	0	15 ⎱	n.a.	n.a.
Two-stage selective	n.a.	n.a.	⎰	⎰	0	0	0	0	⎰	n.a.	n.a.
Package deal	n.a.	n.a.	10	10	0	0	0	0	⎰	n.a.	n.a.

Sources:
a Reference 3
a Reference 4 Table XII
b Reference 7 Table 2
c Reference 10 pp 7-8 and Appendix 1
d Reference 8 Tables 1.16 and 1.17
(E) Author's estimate
f Columns do not always sum to 100 owing to rounding

An attempt is made in Table 7.1 opposite to bring together data from different sources often having slightly different meanings and to interpret it so that work is allocated according to broad categories of type of tender.

The main contractor having been chosen, there is still the question of the type of contract which will be used. For public-sector contracts, Government has been trying as part of its anti-inflationary policy to insist on fixed-price contracts for all contracts under two years' duration. This is shown in the statistics of types of contract for local authority housing,[4] where 97 per cent (1970) of all contracts with contractors have been fixed-price contracts and only 3 per cent contracts with fluctuation clauses. However, as the contracts over two years would be the larger ones, the percentage by value with fluctuation clauses could be higher. Even in the private sector,[3] of all contracts given to contractors 86 per cent were fixed price, 9 per cent fluctuating price and nearly 4 per cent cost plus fee (either fixed or percentage) for factories, and for offices the corresponding figures were 82 per cent, 13 per cent and 4 per cent.

This means that on most contracts contractors are assessing their costs and their price before the contract is executed at then existing prices and, in addition, have to assess how the prices of materials and labour are likely to change over the period of the contract. The whole process is in fact completely reversed from the procedure in most of manufacturing industry. For most products the producer has finally to determine his price only after the good has been produced and his actual costs are known with reasonable certainty, and he controls, subject to competition, the conditions under which his goods are sold. Over most of the construction industry the client not only asks for a fixed price before the goods are produced, but is also the principal party to determine the conditions under which the building is built, i.e. the form of pricing and contract used. In most industries the producer is the person who fixes the terms on which he will do business and the customer has to 'take it or leave it'. In the contracting industry the customer fixes the conditions on which he is prepared to do business, although not the price, and the contractor has to 'take it or leave it'. It is not possible or relevant here to say what it the 'better' system. It is, however, important to realise that it has very substantial effects on the structure of the industry and its functioning.

There are two exceptions to this method of pricing. The first is that in which the contractor is acting as a developer and which for reasons outlined above is excluded from detailed consideration here. The second exception is the appointment of a managing contractor on a fee basis. He will engage other contractors to do the work. This is still relatively unimportant (and is not included in Table 7.1), but many large contractors now offer this service and the practice seems to be growing.

Apart from the main contractor there are a number of subcontractors on construction work who will usually be specialists in one trade or type of work. The Research Services Report (1968)[8] analyses the way in which both large and small* firms of specialist contractors obtain their work. Package deals are relatively unimportant and such as there are would probably be for such highly technical specialisms as heating and ventilating. For the rest, in large firms about 60 per cent is by open tender, another 9 per cent by selective tender, 17 per cent nominated (by the architect or other consultant) and 14 per cent negotiated or serial tender. For small firms the figures are 32 per cent open tender, 18 per cent selective tender, 41 per cent nominated and 10 per cent negotiated or serial tendering. In the case of nomination by the architect the subcontractor nevertheless has his contract with the main contractor.

It is worth noting in passing that the total value of contracts let in the construction industry is greater than the value of the work done on those contracts because the total of work is included in the main contract and then part of it is let again in subcontracts. This may occasionally be important in interpreting figures of tendering procedure, e.g. those in the Phelps Brown (1968)[6] research compared with *Action on the Banwell Report* (1967).[7] It also means that although, say, 15 per cent of work is excluded from consideration here because it is done by constructor/developers, some of the value of this work may be let in subcontracts which are included in the coverage.

*For definition, see footnote to p. 79 above.

WORK LOAD ON THE INDUSTRY

It has been said that as long as the clients of the contracting industry place their demands in such a way that they may require any type of structure at any time in any place, they will get the industry they deserve.

The work put to the construction industry is of extremely varied type and size. It is not necessary here to give a detailed breakdown, which is available elsewhere,[9] but the numerical preponderance of contracts under £50,000 spread over the country is indicative of the need for a very large number of small firms widely distributed geographically. On the other hand, in 1971, 0·3 per cent of the contracts for commercial building were over £2 million in value and these accounted for about £170 million of work or over a quarter of the value of orders for all commercial building. In public non-housing work, the other sector with very large contracts, 0·7 per cent of the jobs accounted for £470 million of work or about 30 per cent of the orders in the whole sector. There was a discussion in Chapter 3 of how far it is realistic to speak of a single industry undertaking work of such different scale and complexity.

The spread of the size of contract with a very large number of small ones and a few very large ones is mirrored in the structure of the industry. Small firms employing 25 persons or fewer in 1970 accounted for about 90 per cent of all firms, and did 23 per cent of the work. Large firms employing 1,200 persons and over accounted for about 0·1 per cent of all firms but did 24 per cent of the work.[4]

The structure of the industry is very complex too in the types of firms split according to their trade. The Department of the Environment distinguishes twenty-two different trades.[4] The very large firms are nearly all building and civil engineering contractors with head offices in London or another large conurbation and with national coverage for large works. The specialist contractors are mostly smaller, but the most important of them may also work all over the country. The great mass of medium-sized and small general building contractors, spread all over the country, have varying areas of operation around their base.*

*The Building Economics Research Unit of the School of Environ-

Research undertaken for the Phelps Brown Committee (1968)[8] showed that each contract normally accounts for an important proportion of the turnover of any one firm. Small companies on average had 10 contracts while medium and large ones had 24. Firms with 300 or more employees claimed an average of 96 contracts. However, it must be borne in mind that large firms may operate in many diverse markets and within each market the number of contracts may be small. This dependence on a few contracts which is a feature of the firms in the industry has important repercussions on the operation of firms.

---

mental Studies, University College, London, is undertaking research into 'The Building Process: The Mechanism of Response to Effective Demand' which may yield some valuable data on catchment areas of contractors.

PART THREE

The Supply of Construction

8 The Firm and its Objectives

In previous chapters the demand on the construction industry has been examined. In the sections on supply the way in which the industry responds to the demand must be analysed, first in terms of the firms which actually carry out the construction work.

Economists use the word 'firm' to mean a business unit. The person who takes the decisions and risks of business is known as the 'entrepreneur'. Whereas at one time the risk-bearer and the decision-maker were usually one and the same, this function is now often divided, for example between the shareholders and the managers.

TYPES OF FIRM

There are many types of firm,* of which the principal are:

The Partnership

This is of importance principally in the professions, where each partner takes unlimited responsibility for the business, and his personal capital can be called upon to pay the debts of the partnership. Such a firm has no recourse to outside funds except on a loan basis. A few professional organisations are becoming limited companies in spite of the fact that this debars them from being members of their professional association. One of the main reasons for their decision is the more favourable tax treatment. Around 10 per cent of construction firms in the United Kingdom are partnerships.[2]

The Private One-man Business

Some small contractors carry on operations in a purely private

*Although in most Western countries the types of firm are similar, these comments refer specifically to the United Kingdom. For further details of the types of firm, see Speight (1967).[1]

capacity using their own capital with unlimited liability. These businesses account for 15–20 per cent of United Kingdom construction firms.[2]

The Limited Liability Company

In limited liability companies shareholders' liability is limited to the money invested. Most of the work of the industry is done by such firms. Within this group of the limited liability company may be distinguished two sub-groups: the private company and the public company.

The private company may not have more than fifty shareholders and is dependent for its finance on investments by its shareholders and on loans from banks and other lending institutions. The shareholders, the owners and the managers are often the same persons. Over 70 per cent of United Kingdom construction companies are in this category.[2]

The public company is able to go to the general public for finance. In exchange for this right, it must give the public more information on its activities and finances. Relatively few companies in the contracting industry are public companies, but they are all large and therefore relatively important in terms of the work they carry out.

The United Kingdom construction industry meets the demands upon it through the actions of a large number – some 70,000 – business units or firms of the various types described above.

In economic theory confusion may arise because in some cases economists refer to the firm to denote the actual business units in existence and in other cases use the term as an abstraction denoting some sort of representative business unit run by a rational entrepreneur who behaves according to a given set of assumptions. Although the theoretical economist postulates the various assumptions on the basis of his belief that they bear a strong resemblance to the firm of the real world, it is sufficient for his purposes if they are adequately representative of the real-world firm, and it is not necessary, in order for the assumptions to be useful, for a majority or even for any of the firms to behave exactly as the theoretical firm, so long as on average they do not diverge too far from it.

OBJECTIVES OF THE FIRM

The traditional objective of the entrepreneur of this theoretical firm is the maximisation of money profits, and this assumption is very strongly entrenched. It still forms the basis of most micro-economic theory, and together with the marginal approach which it embodies, it enables statements to be made – by a process of aggregation – about total market phenomena and equilibrium conditions.

Particularly in the last thirty years, the profit-maximisation approach has been challenged at two levels: the first that, although it is basically akin to reality, there are circumstances in which other objectives play a part; and secondly, on the fundamental level that it bears little real relationship to the way firms actually behave.

At the more trivial level, for example, it is pointed out that there is no reason to suppose that the entrepreneur will, above a certain level of profit, value increases in profit more than increases in his leisure or that his objectives may change from making money to gaining respect and, say, becoming a local dignitary or secretary of the golf club. It is not difficult to accept this comment and still maintain that the overall concept of profit maximisation as the objective is tenable – allowing some idiosyncrasies for the small firm. Even the problem that if a high degree of competition exists, any entrepreneur who does not maximise profit would go out of business, can be overcome by postulating that the level of income which he is prepared to accept is lower than that which he could earn elsewhere. There is also considerable support in the contracting industry for the idea that contracting is a 'way of life' and that many contractors would not wish to cease business even if they could obtain a higher return on their capital and labour by using it in some other way. This is presumably true in one degree or another in a great many industries, for example certainly in agriculture, but the distinct characteristics of construction lead one to suppose that it may be especially true of this industry. It may also be true that many family firms may limit their expansion to maintain the firm at a size manageable within the family. Thus it could be that sometimes the expansion of a family firm is determined by the number of children growing up and wishing to work in it.

The most fundamental attack on profit maximisation comes from the behavioural theorists, of whom Cyert and March (1963)[3] are two. They see the objectives of the firm, mainly the large corporation, as determined by organisational structure and the internal operations of the firm as much as by purely monetary objectives. Between the behavioural theorists and the profit-maximisation school is a large range of opinion and it would be outside the scope of this book to attempt a review, especially as others[4, 5] have gathered together many of the ideas under discussion. There would, however, seem to be a reasonable consensus of opinion that, firstly, the greater the convergence of interests of owner and manager, the greater the likelihood of some approximation to the objective of profit maximisation, and secondly, that the greater the degree of competition, the more important is it for survival that entrepreneurs aim at profit maximisation. It must be considered how far these conditions exist in the construction industry.

In a high proportion of firms of the construction industry, the owner or part-owner of the firm is in an executive position. Research carried out for the Bolton Committee[2] showed that over 84 per cent of the chief executives were the founder or members of the founder's family – a rather higher figure than for most manufacturing industry but lower than for much non-manufacturing industry. This general statement has, however, to be seen against the background of the structure of the industry in which the 79 large firms (1970) employing more than 1,200 operatives do 23 per cent of the work and small firms employing 25 operatives or less and accounting for 90 per cent of all firms also do 23 per cent of the work.[6] It is clear that if the 16 per cent where the chief executive was not a member of the founder's family were all large, the argument of substantial overlap of ownership and control would disappear. Although for the great majority of firms there is no split of interest, it would still be possible that for the great mass of the work done interests would be divided. There is, however, some other evidence. An examination of some ten of the largest companies shows that in most of them the founder or a member of the founder's family is on the board, usually as chairman or managing director.

The degree of competition in the construction industry is discussed at some length in Chapter 12, and the conclusions reached are that the industry has many attributes of competition and of oligopoly, and that the balance depends on the situation in the individual markets. In general, however, the firms in the industry see themselves as competing very hard against other firms – there is certainly 'effective' competition.

As far as the author is aware, no survey data are available on the extent to which contractors aim to maximise revenue or profits,* and the uncertainties of the estimating and tendering process may mean that the question is not one which the entrepreneurs ask themselves. Familiarity with the industry suggests that while the top management of large contractors and the management of small contractors are aware of the dangers of obtaining work at too low a price, yet within the firm the individual operating units see their success not only in terms of profit, but also in terms of turnover. Clearly, any turnover target must have some minimum level of profit associated with it.

Sir Maurice Laing, speaking on 'Ethics and Conduct of Designers and Constructors' at a meeting of the Joint Building Group on 21 February 1968, referred to the many responsibilities of a large contracting company: to the shareholders for their provision of capital and for the risks they undertake, it owes a reasonable financial return and growth; to the employees for their vital hard work, loyalty and initiative, it owes a financially sound business to pay adequate remuneration, congenial, rewarding, safe, regular and secure work, training to enable employees to use their abilities to the full, an up-to-date progressive policy on conditions of employment and treatment of employees with humanity and equity; to the client for the business he provides and the trust he bestows, it owes a good service at a competitive, realistic price and the duty to be sure that the client is fully aware of the product and service which he can expect for that price; to the subcontractors and suppliers it owes fair dealing; to the community it owes a satisfactory environment when it is in its power to provide it and responsibility

*A survey, at present in the pilot stage, by the Building Economics Research Unit at University College, London, may yield some of these data.

to use resources – human resources in particular – efficiently and effectively.

Most of these objectives are not quantifiable, although they should clearly be considered in any policy of the firm. On the matter of profits and growth, which are of more particular interest for the theory of the firm, he said that for the widely held public company 'the primary objective must be financial and that this is to make adequate profits.... The second objective for such a company must be to remain in business. The third, I suggest, is to progress and expand for the benefit of the shareholders.'

Sir Maurice's philosophy is not inconsistent with that of Brech (1971)[7] in his discussion of the objectives of the construction firm. He too sees many responsibilities of the firm, but puts the profit objective in perspective, while not in any way diminishing its importance in business.

OBJECTIVES CONSIDERED IN THIS BOOK

In the discussion on the operation of the firm which follows, the implications of two objectives will be considered.

The first and the most heavily weighted will be that of profit maximisation. This seems to be reasonable on the following grounds: firstly, it is probably the assumption having the closest approximation to average behaviour in the construction industry; secondly, firms must make profits (in the accountancy sense) and hence it makes sense to see on what profits depend; thirdly, profit maximisation and the marginal approach enable some statements to be made about the market situation for which other theory is as yet not developed. Fourthly, although in capitalist countries the profit motive is not always regarded as the efficient allocator of resources which it is supposed to be, in socialist countries it is being reinstated as a measure of efficiency of units of production in their use of resources and often as a method of allocating resources within limited areas of activity (Gloushkov, 1969).[8] This suggests that it is of some value in achieving national efficiency.

The measure of profit in which the entrepreneur is primarily interested is the return on capital employed, firstly because it is this which the owners of the firm require, and secondly because it is this profit which should be compared to the returns on capital in alternative uses, such as in other industries or in fixed-interest securities. In the analysis which follows, however, profit is often considered in relation to turnover. Maximum profit on turnover will produce maximum profit on capital only if the ratio of capital to turnover is the same in all the various parts of the enterprise. In fact there is quite a substantial difference in the number of times per annum that contractors can turn over their capital, and constant efforts are needed to control capital in use. However, with this reservation, a consideration of the profit in relation to costs and price and of these in relation to output yields a reasonable indication of profitability.

The second objective to be considered is that of making a normal profit or some other minimum level of profit and thereafter seeking maximisation of turnover. This assumption seems to meet some of the problems of different objectives of owners and managers, and it is not difficult to see how the conclusions for profit maximisation would be altered by this alternative assumption.

9 Costs of the Construction Firm

TYPES OF COST RELATIONSHIP

One of the peculiarities of the construction industry is that work is obtained in the form of contracts for projects which are large and indivisible but that the work load relating to each project is spread over a long period of time. Costs (and revenue: see Chapter 12) have therefore to be examined in three distinct ways. The first is the cost of the project as a whole; secondly, the cost of the total project must be related to the work load over time; and lastly, the cost of various alternative work loads at a given point in time must be analysed. The usual cost curves of economic analysis are of this last type. The method of transition from the first to the third will be discussed first.

Fig. 9.1 shows the estimated total cost of the contracts received at various dates and the period of time over which the work will be carried out. Usually the work on a contract builds up over time first slowly and then more rapidly to a peak and then declines, first quickly and then slowly, prior to final completion. However, for simplicity of exposition it is assumed here that work is spread evenly over the period of the contract starting in the month following the order. Thus contract (1) for £12 million obtained in January and lasting 60 months costs £200,000 a month from February to December in the same year. Contract (2) for £2 million in April spread over 20 months costs £100,000 a month from May to December, and together contracts (1) and (2) have a cost shown by the line *ABCK* in Fig. 9.2. Two other contracts obtained in the year lead to a cumulative cost curve for all four contracts of *ABCDEFGH*. At the same time there will be work going on from contracts obtained in previous years and this is represented by the stepped dotted line from *L* to *M*. Altogether the cost of work over the year is shown by the top line from *L* to *H*. Thus the extremely erratic discontinuous new contracts situation yields a less erratic continuous cost curve over time, although still with substantial ups and downs.

If a month is taken as a sufficiently short period of time to be regarded as a 'point in time' over which the usual cost curves of the firm in economic analysis are relevant, in the month of

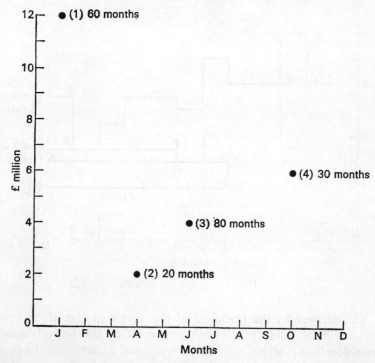

FIG. 9.1 Contracts obtained during the year

June the firm would be at a point on its cost curve shown by the point *N* in Fig. 9.2, with an output of £500,000 units of work and a cost of £500,000. For simplicity, let the £500,000 of units of work be regarded as units of output at a unit cost of £100,000. The question to which the firm requires an answer is: how would the cost be affected if, instead of producing 5 units in June, it was producing a larger or smaller amount? This is a very relevant question to the contracting firm because the output in June is partly determined far in advance and therefore is something which the firm can hope to control and yet, for reasons described later in this chapter under the heading of 'Uncertainty in Work Load', it may have a higher or lower output thrust upon it by circumstances outside its control.

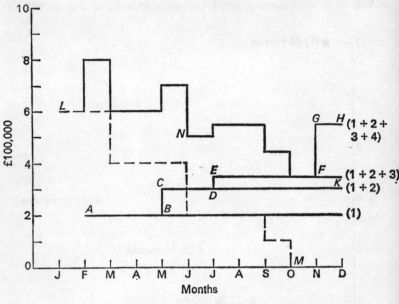

FIG. 9.2. Costs per month

The answer to the question of the shape of the firm's cost curve will be different according to whether the period under consideration is short, so that the overhead expenses and hence facilities of the firm cannot be altered, or whether the period is so long that the whole structure of the firm and the level of technology at which it operates can be adjusted. Moreover the answer will be different according to the work mix of the changed work load. It could be that a higher or lower output is achieved either by changing the average size of contract and keeping the number of contracts constant or by changing the number of contracts and keeping average size of contract constant. In practice of course there will probably be a combination of the two, but for analytical purposes it is useful to consider the two extremes. In the discussion of inputs of site construction and the contracting firm which follow, attention is concentrated first on the relatively short-term position in which the expenses at head office are fixed and the supply of certain site management is fixed. Inputs are divided into three categories: variable, i.e. those which vary directly with the value of output and which must be covered in the short run; fixed, i.e. those whose level cannot be altered in the period under review but which must be covered if the enterprise as a whole is not to make a loss; and postponable costs, i.e. those which must be covered in the very long run but need not be covered in the short run. It will be assumed in the analysis that, apart from variations in size and number of contracts, the type of work done by the firm can be expressed in homogeneous units. It is also assumed that the level of output from which divergence is being considered is within a band of optimum or near-optimum combinations of resources for their level of output. Table 9.1 summarises the broad conclusions derived from the discussion below under each input of the changes in the level of output. Costs are expressed in terms of cost per unit of output. If total cost changes in proportion to output, then the costs per unit of output will be the same. If total cost rises by more than the output, costs per unit of output will rise, and if total cost rises less than proportionately to output, then costs per unit of output will fall. These relationships are discussed more fully under the heading of 'Short-run Total Cost Curve and the Derivation of Average and Marginal Cost Curves' (p. 104 below).

VARIABLE COSTS

Materials Used on Site

Materials and components used on site account for rather under half the total cost of construction. In broad terms the cost of materials will vary directly with the amount of work under way. There might be some exceptions to this at extremely low sizes of contract because of the lower limit to the quantity in which certain materials can be bought, the non-availability for small purchases of quantity discounts and the possibility that central purchasing may not be worth while. If the number of contracts is small, the size remaining the same, the effect of small outputs

TABLE 9.1

Change in Short-run Unit Costs below and above Output at or near Optimum Level of Output

	Change in output by change in size of contracts		Change in output by change in number of contracts	
	Below optimum	Above optimum	Below optimum	Above optimum
Variable costs				
1. Materials used on site	Higher	Same then higher with management inefficiency	Same or higher if no bulk buying	Same then higher with management inefficiency
2. Labour used on site	Higher	Higher with over-time and management inefficiency	Same	Same then higher with management inefficiency
3. Some site management	Same	Same	Same	Same
4. Plant and equipment on site	Same	Same	Same	Same
5. Interest on working capital for site work	Same	Same	Same	Same
6. Estimating costs assuming constant ratio of successful bids	Same	Same	Same	Same
Fixed costs				
7. Employees at head office including contracts and some site managers	Higher	Lower	Higher	Lower
8. Outgoings on buildings and equipment	Higher	Lower	Higher	Lower
9. Minimum level of remuneration of entrepreneur	Higher	Lower	Higher	Lower
10. Interest on loans if not postponable	Higher	Lower	Higher	Lower
Postponable costs				
11. Normal remuneration over minimum of entrepreneur	Higher	Lower	Higher	Lower
12. Normal return on capital which can be withdrawn	Higher	Lower	Higher	Lower

on costs of materials is likely to be negligible unless the low turnover implies the abandonment of central bulk buying.

Assuming that at the original output there was already centralised buying and that quantity discounts were obtained, then higher levels of output either with more contracts or larger contracts should not affect the unit cost of materials until the point is reached where the management of the project becomes inefficient owing to fixity of some management skills leading to wastage and damage of materials and components.

Labour Used on Site

Site labour accounts for about a third of the cost of construction. Much site labour in the construction industry is employed for one project only, particularly in large firms and for large contracts. Hence in broad terms the cost of labour will vary with the amount of work under way. At low sizes of contract, however, there may be specialist craftsmen who are not fully employed all the time although their presence is necessary and therefore labour costs may be proportionately higher. At high contract sizes and great intensity of work on site with a large amount of work crammed into a short space of time there will probably be inefficient use of manpower with too short a period of time as a buffer against some operations taking longer than anticipated. If gangs cannot see sufficient work ahead of them, they tend to work more slowly than if they know that they can move on to the next operation. Disruption will also probably occur owing to the intensity of work and the inadequacy of planning and management of work and men. Lastly, the unit cost of labour may well rise with overtime rates. There will also be the additional cost of recruitment. For all these reasons the cost of labour at higher levels of output is likely to rise by more than the amount of work carried out.

If the expansion of the firm is attained not by larger contracts but by more of them at higher outputs and fewer of them at low outputs, the differences in cost of labour will depend on the quality of site management. Two broad divisions of costs have been made into those arising at head office, i.e. overheads, and those arising on site. If it is possible to expand the supply of site management by recruitment of the same calibre of managers and foremen, etc., as used on existing work and at the same price, then labour on each site should be organised to the same degree of efficiency and there should be no increase in costs. If, however, the supply of efficient site management is difficult to expand quickly, then the efficiency of the whole site will decline and this will show itself partly in higher labour costs. It has been assumed in Table 9.1 and under 'Site Management' below that some site management is variable while part is fixed. In these circumstances there would be some decreases in efficiency at high levels of output with more contracts.

Site Management

Management in the construction industry is remarkably mobile. It is therefore assumed that a large part of management can be recruited at short notice and is therefore a variable cost. There is, however, some senior site management which remains with a company on a long-term basis and to which the company feels some obligation to offer security of employment. This type of site management is assumed to be in fixed supply just as is the staff employed at head office.

There seems no particular reason why it should be expected that the cost of variable site management would not rise roughly in proportion to the work done. In the case of large contracts, personnel in charge would be paid a higher salary, and in the case of a larger number of contracts management personnel would be duplicated. In any case the absolute cost of management is relatively small in relation to the total cost of the contract.

The effect and importance of management lies not in the direct costs but in the effect it has on the efficiency of the whole project and hence on labour costs, and even on material and plant costs. This is particularly relevant as management expertise is one of the scarcest resources of the construction industry in the United Kingdom, in many other developed countries and certainly in developing countries.

Plant and Equipment on Site

Plant and equipment used on site may be hired or owned. If it is hired its cost is the hire fee. If it is owned its cost has two components: that which is dependent on the extent to which it is used, i.e. depreciation which varies with intensity of production, and that which depends on the rate at which it becomes obsolete. Its capital cost should be recouped over the total contracts for which the equipment is used. If, as is the case on many large contracts, the item of plant and equipment is worn out during that contract, then the whole of the cost has to be related to that particular contract. If it is used over several contracts, then the cost not due to its use is more properly considered as a fixed cost.

The amount of plant used will increase with size of contract, but there is little evidence to indicate whether or not it will increase proportionately. However, data from the Census of Industrial Production (1969)[1] show no significant increase in the percentage of capital expenditure of gross output as the size of firm increases. As the size of firm is fairly closely correlated with the average size of contract, this gives some indication that an assumption of a change in plant costs proportionate to output is not unrealistic for output changes with constant and changing sizes of contract.

Working Capital for Site Work

Working capital or any other finance is not a resource of construction in the same way as, say, materials or labour. Indeed, if the money invested were added to the other inputs this would result in double counting, because if it is invested it is always in some physical resource which would have been considered in any case. Nevertheless, it is necessary for the construction firm to be able to use resources before they are paid for, and the interest paid on working capital is the cost of this facility.

The normal method of payment for construction contracts is that once a month the architect or other professional adviser to the client certifies the value of the work which has been done on site and the client pays the contractor the amount of the certificate minus a small percentage which is retained until after the end of the contract in case of defects in the work. The contractor needs working capital to pay for material, labour, etc., from the time of commencement of work or from the date of the last certificate until the date of the next certificate, plus the period between the date of the certificate and his receipt of payment. There is room for considerable skill in keeping this

working capital to a very low figure by, for example, the use
of credit from builders' merchants and other methods outside
the scope of this book. There may even be instances where the
contractor manages to ensure that his cash receipts exceed his
cash outgoings, in which case working capital required is negative. Normally, however, it is positive and its cost will be the
rate of interest he has to pay on it (or the forgone interest if he
is using his own capital). The actual sum involved is negligible
in most contracts compared with the cost of labour and materials.

The importance of working capital in the industry is, however, very great, not on account of its cost but because contractors may be unable to obtain sufficient working capital at any
price. This is mentioned later in a consideration of the rate at
which construction firms can grow.

Costs of Estimating

Assuming a constant success rate, estimating costs are probably more or less proportionate to the value of the work obtained, whether in large or small contracts. For this reason they
are included under variable costs, although estimators are normally part of the head office establishment. After the business
has been obtained, however, they are fixed costs because, as
was mentioned in Chapter 7, the cost of estimating for successful and unsuccessful tenders is borne by the successful tenders.
The higher the success rate in bidding, the lower the costs of
estimating which have to be added to each contract.

FIXED COSTS

These are a relatively small proportion of total costs of a construction firm and have been taken to be the expenses incurred
at head office, plus obsolescence and depreciation not related
directly to use of plant whose life extends over more than one
project, and site management which is difficult to recruit easily
and for whom the business offers security of employment. It will
include too a minimum level of remuneration for the entrepreneur as well as interest on loans, other than those already considered for site working capital, the payment of which cannot be
postponed.

Since these costs are all by definition regarded as fixed, i.e. they do not vary with the amount of work undertaken, they will be lower per unit of output the higher the level of output and vice versa, irrespective of whether the output is in large, medium or small contracts. This is shown in Table 9.1.

The remuneration of the owners of the firm who are working in the firm is often considered as a part of profit by accountants. Economists consider normal profits, i.e. that profit which is just enough to keep the entrepreneur in the industry, as a long-run cost of the business. This normal profit would be closely related to that which he could earn elsewhere, although not necessarily synonymous with it for reasons discussed in Chapter 8. However, it will normally be larger for the more efficient producers than for the less efficient ones. In the short run, however, the entrepreneur would usually be prepared to stay in the industry for considerably less than normal profit. If he had no other earnings he would, however, presumably need some minimum level of remuneration, and it is this which is included in fixed costs.

In the case of fixed investment in plant and buildings the problem of the difference between the physical assets and the financial position arises again. Fixed investment in the buildings and equipment which is already owned by the firm is in the short run at least a sunk cost (see Chapter 3), i.e. a cost which need not be included. However, the extent to which this is so in practice depends on how the physical assets are financed. If they are financed by loans on which interest payments cannot be postponed, then the interest charges must be included and this will be a fixed cost, since it has already been assumed that in the short run it cannot be altered. If on the other hand it is, for example, financed out of equity capital on which there is no obligation to pay any return, then the cost can be postponed. Similar arguments apply to the working capital required.

POSTPONABLE COSTS

Costs which may be postponed are that part of the normal remuneration of the entrepreneur which is not required by him to maintain him and his family (which is a fixed cost) and the normal return on all capital invested in the business apart from that on which interest has to be regularly paid. If the entrepreneur is content to allow the business to remain at its present size or is incapable of expanding it, then only the normal return on capital which can be withdrawn from the business must be met. The remainder is a sunk cost which does not affect the operation of the business at its present level. In the long run, if the business is to expand the whole of both these must be met because otherwise it will not be possible to obtain further finance for expansion. If no return is accruing to existing equity capital, the public will not be prepared to provide any more of it.

The entrepreneur is unlikely to regard the profit which he should earn to keep himself in the industry as directly proportionate to output, but it seems likely that when the business expands to a higher level of work and employs more expensive specialists he will feel that he is now in charge of a business of a different type and will set his sights higher so far as his own remuneration is concerned. Thus it is likely to go up in a step fashion. In the short run, however, he will accept a fixed level.

The normal return on capital in the long run is also likely to go up in step fashion as the investment is unlikely to expand smoothly, e.g. expenditure on a new office block comes as a large once-and-for-all expenditure. However, in the short run it has been assumed to be fixed.

SHORT-RUN TOTAL COST CURVE AND THE DERIVATION OF AVERAGE AND MARGINAL COST CURVES

From the discussion above it is apparent that the total short-run variable cost of producing low levels of output is fairly high, lower at medium levels and may then increase more than proportionately to increases in output because of the fixity in the short run of the supply of certain types of management and the facilities provided by head office. Table 9.2, column (3) shows how variable total costs might change with the level of output, and this is shown in graphical form in Fig. 9.3A by curve *TCV*. The values of the changes shown probably exaggerate the extent of the variability in the normal firm but have been shown in this way for ease of exposition. The general shape of the curve is, however, realistic.

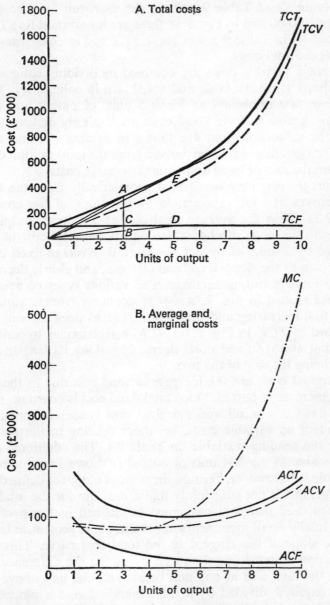

FIG. 9.3. Short-run costs of the firm

Column (2) of Table 9.2 shows the short-run fixed costs as being £100,000 and in Fig. 9.3A these are the straight line *TCF*. Column (4) in Table 9.2 and curve *TCT* in Fig. 9.3A show the sum of the total costs.

Average variable costs are obtained by dividing column (3) by column (1) in the table and are shown in column (6). They decrease to a minimum at 4 and 5 units of output and then increase again. Average fixed costs are similarly derived from columns (2) and (1) and are shown in column (5), and total average costs may either be derived from the total of total costs or from the sum of fixed and variable average costs.

Average costs may be derived geometrically from the total cost curves and are represented by the slope of the cord in Fig. 9.3A. Thus the average total cost at 3 units of output is shown in the slope of *OA*, which equals the total cost of 346 divided by 3 units of output $=$ AB/OB. Average fixed costs are shown by the slope of *OC* and *OD*, etc., and clearly decrease as the units of output increase. The various types of average cost are plotted in Fig. 9.3B: *ACV* denoting average variable costs first increasing and then decreasing, as does the slope of the cord of *TCV* in Fig. 9.3A; *ACF*, a rectangular hyperbola, denoting average fixed costs decreasing along its length; and *ACT* being the sum of the two.

Marginal costs are the increase in total cost due to the last small increase in output. Since total fixed cost is constant, marginal fixed cost is nil and marginal cost is therefore entirely dependent on variable costs, i.e. those relating to the project under the heading 'variable' in Table 9.1. The additional cost attributable to the last unit of output is shown in column (8) of Table 9.2. However, because the units of output as defined are so large, this is not sufficiently fine a measure for the analysis required, and marginal cost must be defined in terms of infinitesimally small increments in output, i.e. in geometric terms by the slope of the tangent to the total cost curve. This has been approximated in column (9) by taking the difference between the total cost at one unit below and one unit above the point required, divided by 2. This marginal cost is plotted in Fig. 9.3B, and is at its lowest at output 3. It is also clear that the slope of the cord and the slope of the tangent to the total cost curve in Fig. 9.3A are the same at output 5, i.e. at *E*, and

TABLE 9.2
Short-run Total Average and Marginal Costs of the Firm
(£'000)

(1) Output	Total costs (2) Fixed	(3) Variable	(4) Total	Average costs (5) Fixed	(6) Variable	(7) Total	Marginal costs (8) Extra cost of 1 unit	(9) Smoothed marginal
0	100	0	100	—	—	—	—	—
1	100	90	190	100	90	190	90	85
2	100	170	270	50	85	135	80	78
3	100	246	346	33	82	115	76	75
4	100	320	420	25	80	105	74	77
5	100	400	500	20	80	100	80	101
6	100	522	622	17	87	104	122	122·5
7	100	665	765	14	95	109	143	183
8	100	888	988	12·5	111	123·5	223	266
9	100	1,197	1,297	11	133	144	309	381
10	100	1,640	1,740	10	164	174	453	566

this is the point at which the cord has its lowest slope. On Fig. 9.3B this is where the marginal cost curve and the average total cost curve cut. Thus the marginal cost curve always cuts the average cost curve at the latter's lowest point.

It will be noted that at 5 units of output the average total cost is £100,000. These are the figures which relate to the output of the contracting firm in June derived from Figs. 9.1 and 9.2. Thus the question posed at this stage as to what the costs would be at outputs above and below this level has been answered by the general shape of the cost curves in Figs. 9.3A–B.

Three general rules as to the relationship between marginal cost and average cost may be stated: (i) when the average cost curve is falling, the marginal cost must be below it; (ii) marginal cost equals average cost when average cost is at its lowest; and (iii) when average cost is rising, marginal cost must be above average cost. Thus total, average and marginal costs are ways of expressing the overall cost situation. The one which is chosen for discussion at any time will depend on the nature of the analysis being undertaken.

DIFFERENCE BETWEEN TRADITIONAL AND INDUSTRIALISED CONSTRUCTION

The general relationships assumed in these diagrams apply to the contracting firm undertaking traditional construction work. If, however, the firm is in the business of industrialised construction, e.g. housing, schools, hospitals or factories, it will have cost relationships more akin to manufacturing industry. Fixed costs will be a much higher proportion of total costs. This means that at small levels of output the fixed-cost element will be very high and the slope of the average cost curve before the lowest average cost will be much greater. Variable costs will be correspondingly less important. Thus so long as the firm is not producing at full manufacturing production capacity, average variable costs are likely to decrease or increase only slowly even if there is some increase in variable costs due to the fixity of management, etc., in the short run. When the firm is approaching full manufacturing capacity, i.e. the maximum sustainable output per unit of time, it may be able in the short run to increase output by increasing overtime and by some neglect of repairs. For this increase in output, however, variable costs are likely to rise quite steeply. There will come a point when the plant simply cannot produce a larger output, and beyond that point the cost curves of the firm in the short run will be quite irrelevant. There is no such absolute cut-off limit for contracting firms because for quite large ranges of output management can be stretched, and in any case the variable inputs, being such a large proportion, can be increased to obtain a larger output. As has been indicated, however, the cost of such an extension of output may be considerable.

UNCERTAINTY IN WORK LOAD

In a firm where most of the work is obtained on the basis of tenders, it is not possible to anticipate very far in advance exactly what proportion of the tenders put in will be successful. In each company there will be a generally assumed level of, say, 1 in 5 or 1 in 10. A recent study of selected firms in the industry (Lea *et al.*, 1972)[2] found that 'tendering success rates of the firms varied between 17 per cent and 27 per cent by number of bids and between £14 and £40 per £100 of the work bid for'. The success rate can change quickly because of external changes in the market situation not anticipated by the firm or by a small change in policy on the part of the firm itself. If this happens, its actual output may be different from that planned and the number of contracts, which is one of the major determinants of management needs, will rise (or fall) faster still. Thus it is relatively easy for a contracting company to reach the level of rapidly increasing short-run average and marginal costs 'by mistake'. The danger of this arising will be greater, the greater the ratio of tenders put in to tenders accepted and the smaller the number of contracts normally undertaken at any one time. On the second count small firms would suffer most (see Chapter 7). Large and small main contractors, other than dwelling specialists, have a similar reliance on tender work (Research Services Ltd, 1968).[3] If, however, the contractor, instead of increasing his success rate, decreases it, he will be forced back along his cost curve and his average costs will rise. In this case the cost curve will rise faster with smaller outputs because the lower the success rate in bidding, the higher the costs of estimating which have to be added to each contract.

NON-REVERSIBILITY OF COST CURVES

The short-run cost curve is intended to show the effect on costs of *being at* various levels of output, assuming that the time period is too short to do anything about certain fixed items. In fact, however, the extra cost of increasing output by a given percentage and the reduction in cost due to decreasing output by the same percentage may not be identical. There are, for example, costs of recruiting labour in advertisements, management time for selection, a period in which the man recruited is adjusting himself to the new job, etc. Some of these are virtually a form of fixed cost specific to recruitment, but they are marginal to the expansion process as a whole. They are plotted in Fig. 9.4 at *AB*. They are high when few men are employed

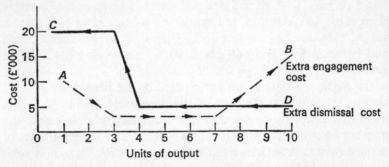

FIG. 9.4. Non-reversible marginal cost curves due to extra costs of engagement or dismissal

and rise again as more effort is required to obtain manpower as labour becomes scarce.

There are also costs in dismissing a man, and with the Redundancy Payments Act if he had been in the employ of the firm for more than two years these costs may be considerable.*

*The Phelps Brown Committee found that the mean of redundancy payments made was £75 for large firms and £96 for small firms (*Research Report*, p. 26). However, many more payments were made in large and medium firms than in small firms.[4]

It has been assumed in curve *CD* that the men dismissed first are not entitled to any redundancy pay, while some of those dismissed later are so entitled. These costs must be added to the original marginal cost curve to obtain a marginal cost curve for increases in output and then for decreases in output.

There will be similar cases of non-reversibility of curves with, for example, the purchase of new plant and the sale of second-hand plant or of materials from the manufacturer and of surplus materials.

PROBLEM OF ACCURATE ESTIMATION OF COSTS

In Chapter 13 the problem that the firm does not know its costs in advance is covered in more detail. It is, however, important here to realise that the level of the cost curve of the firm at any stage is subject to a wide margin of error. This can cause some wrong decisions, and indeed does do so, as is often seen by the wide difference between expected and actual profit. It does not, however, invalidate the analysis, which can be repeated with a 'band' of costs.

LONG-RUN COSTS

There are two meanings of 'short run' as opposed to 'long run', namely the short run as the period in which certain costs are postponable and the short run as the period in which fixed plant and equipment and the head office organisation cannot be altered. The two categories overlap, since some postponable costs have only to be met in the long run if the level of fixed costs is to be altered. It is, however, helpful to consider their effects on the long-run situation separately.

Postponable costs have been isolated in Table 9.1 as the remaining part of the normal remuneration of the entrepreneur, i.e. that necessary to keep him in the business and the normal return on capital which can be withdrawn. In the short run capital was taken as given and it was assumed that the entrepreneur would not in a short period raise his required level of remuneration, and therefore these had the characteristics of fixed costs. In the slightly longer period these costs are not postponable, otherwise the entrepreneur and the capital will be withdrawn from the business. Moreover, in the still longer term the entrepreneur will wish to raise his level of remuneration more in keeping with the volume of business he is handling. Lastly, if fixed costs are increased, then the normal rate of return on the equity capital which cannot be withdrawn becomes relevant, for unless it is paid further capital will not be forthcoming.

Thus in the first use of the phrase 'long-term', i.e. the sense in which costs are no longer postponable, the difference between the long-run cost curve and the short-run cost curve would be that fixed costs are higher. They are also likely to be stepped to take account of the increase required by the entrepreneur in the return on his labours.

In the second use of the expression 'long-term', fixed costs may be increased in combination with a change in technology or simply by, say, doubling the quantity of all inputs of the business. In practice the latter is unlikely, since as a business grows in size it becomes more economical to change the proportion and types of inputs. Attention must now be focused on the possibilities of various technologies and the effects of various levels of fixed costs.

ISO-PRODUCT CURVES*

In the long-run, all the costs which are fixed in the short run become variable costs and, hence, costs of building can be considered in terms of the right combinations of inputs to produce, at various relationships in input prices, the most economical method of production. In Fig. 9.5, *AB* shows all technically possible combinations of capital and manpower which can produce 10 units of output. It is an iso-product curve. The curve has many of the characteristics of indifference curves and may be used in much the same way. Thus, point *C* shows that 10 units of output can be produced with 6 units of manpower and $4\frac{1}{4}$ of capital; point *D* that it can be produced by 5 of manpower

---

*Iso-product curves can also be used in the analysis of the short-term situation by considering the effects when the amount of one input is held constant. This is well covered in the literature.

and 5 of capital. It can also be produced by 4 units of manpower and 6 of capital at *E*, and at point *F* it can be produced by 3 of manpower and 8 of capital. It is clear that in substitution of capital for units of manpower, increasing amounts of capital are required with each unit reduction in manpower. This is known as an increasing rate of marginal substitution. There is a technical limit to the extent to which it is possible to replace manpower by capital, i.e. in order to produce 10 units of output the absolute minimum labour requirement is $1\frac{1}{2}$ units and the

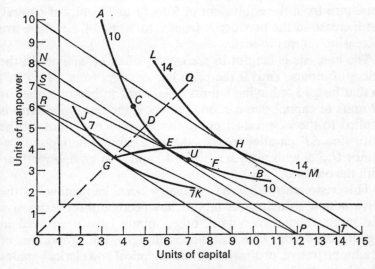

Fig. 9.5. Iso-product curves

iso-product curve 10 becomes asymptotic to the capital axis at $1\frac{1}{2}$. There is similarly a minimum requirement of 1 unit of capital. There will be iso-product curves for each level of output such as *JK* and *LM*. (It will be noted that, unlike indifference curves, these iso-products can be given a quantitative value. It is possible to measure units of output but not units of satisfaction.) The optimum combination of inputs to produce the output of 10 units with a price relationship of 8 units of manpower costing the same as 12 units of capital and a total expenditure equal to 12 units of capital is given at point *E*, because the price line *NP* is tangential to *AB* at *E*. Thus at *E* the technical marginal rate of substitution is equal to the price ratio and, given the fixed total expenditure, is the combination giving the greatest possible output.

There will be a similar optimum point at this price ratio but with different expenditure and outputs at *G* and *H*. The curve *GEH* is the expansion path, i.e. given the prices of inputs, the way in which the firm should expand is by processes which use the combinations of inputs along *GEH*. Because the curve *GEH* has a slope lower than the slope of *OGQ*, as the firm gets bigger it pays to use a higher proportion of capital to manpower. The line *GEH* also shows that with a constant increase in expenditure from the equivalent of 9 to 12 to 15 units of capital, the increase in the product is from 7 to 10 to 14, i.e. there are increasing returns to scale.

The analysis is helpful in seeing the effect of changes in the prices of inputs. Thus if the price line changes from *NP* to *RP*, so that instead of buying 8 units of labour for the same price as 12 units of capital one can buy only 6, if the new price ratio is applied to the iso-product curve for 10 units of output by the price line *ST* parallel to *RP*, the new equilibrium point becomes *U*, i.e. with a higher ratio of capital to manpower than with the old price.

This represents what has actually been happening in the construction industry. As labour has become more expensive and more difficult to obtain, other inputs have been used in higher proportion. One instance is the growing proportion of of administrative, professional, and technical and clerical grades who have made construction more management-intensive in order to increase the product of the site operatives. The main example is the switch from conventional construction methods to industrialised building, as outlined in Chapter 3. There it was found that as labour became more expensive and more difficult to get in relation to other factors of production, it was replaced by capital, and the capital-intensive methods gradually became more economical than the labour-intensive methods.

EFFECT OF DIFFERENT TECHNOLOGIES WITH DIFFERENT
FIXED COSTS

One of the problems of the use of iso-product curves in construction (and presumably in most other industries) is that the tech-

nical possibilities of various combinations of inputs tend to
present themselves in large lumps of variation, in capital for
example, and not as a choice situation where small variations
in capital are feasible. Consequently it is appropriate to consider the technical possibilities as in Fig. 9.6, where three levels
of fixed investment are considered as represented by FC_1, FC_2
and FC_3. Each level of fixed cost is related to a variable cost
curve (not illustrated) and hence to a total cost curve – TC_1,
TC_2 and TC_3 respectively. It is apparent that in this highly
simplified situation the solid curved line $ABCD$ is that showing
the lowest possible cost, and hence the different technologies
and their related fixed costs should be introduced at $8\frac{1}{2}$ units
of output and 13 units of output respectively.

It is interesting to note that at point B the same output can
be produced at the same cost with two completely different
levels of fixed costs and technologies. This explains why firms
of two widely different sizes and organisations can compete
effectively for the same contract.

Fig. 9.6 is in fact an over-simplification. Firstly, any investment in fixed plant and equipment will entail the lapse of time
from the moment of decision to the moment of operation. This

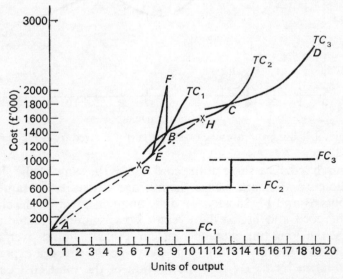

FIG. 9.6. Long-run total cost curves with varying fixed costs

period will have costs, some of them substantial. Thus there would probably be a step in the long-run cost curve, at, say, *EFB*, as expenditure on the new plant developed. Secondly, in fact the enterprise will probably be unable to caculate exactly the value of the point *B*. It may be preferable to make the investment too early rather than too late, because if it is made too late some potential demand may be turned away to rivals and be lost for a long period. For this reason too the cost curve may be stepped as the firm moves to different technologies.

From the long-run cost curve *ABCD* may be derived the average long-run cost curve of the firm in which technologies

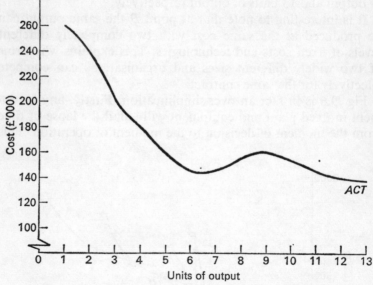

FIG. 9.7. Long-run average total cost curves derived from Fig. 9.6

are not fixed. The slope of the cord at *G* is the same as the slope of the cord at *H* and hence the average costs are the same at outputs $6\frac{1}{2}$ and 11. In between these outputs, however, the slope of the cord and hence the average cost is much greater and hence the long-run average cost curve has a hump over this range. This is shown in Fig. 9.7 – ignoring the effect of expenditure shown by *EFB* – for the portion of the total cost curve *ABC*.

There are in practice a very large number of indivisible items which cause discontinuous changes in fixed costs which, with non-linear variable total costs, can cause humps in the long-run average cost curve of the firm. At the very lowest level a spade, for example, is not a useful implement at all if it is below a certain size, nor is a concrete-mixer or a crane. On the management side, the degree of specialised knowledge is such that it is barely possible to have a half-time project planner (unless his services are brought in as a consultant, in which case his cost will be high). Similarly, a research department has to be of a certain minimum size before it is a viable unit. Because of the 'lumpiness' of some factor of production there will be certain stretches of the long-term cost curve which have some of the characteristics of the short-term cost curve. On a log scale of output it might conceptually look something like the diagram in Fig. 9.8.

Clearly, as the output of the firm increases, the disrupting element would have to become larger and larger before it significantly affected the shape of the average cost curve, and on this diagrammatic presentation only a few of the possible changes have been shown. It was, however, deliberate to bunch some of these elements around 10 output units, because it is often considered by persons in the industry that there is a major point of crisis in a firm's growth when it is too big for the directors of the firm to control each project without some further expertise and too small to afford this expertise. This area is shown here around 10 output units. The real value of the 10 output units will differ according to the type of market the firm is operating in as well as to the calibre of the existing management. It is most usually considered to be in the size group employing, say, between 100 and 300, and certainly in the Department of the Environment[5] category of firms employing 115 to 299 persons, the average number of administrative, professional, technical and clerical staff employed roughly trebles compared with the previous two size groups, while the size of firm measured by persons employed has doubled or less than doubled. The disproportionate increase in administrative, professional, technical and clerical staff compared with size of firm continues in the higher size groups. Turin (1972)[6] has found that the proportion of administrative, professional, technical and clerical staff as a percentage of the total staff grows roughly in proportion with the log of the size of firms.

Apart from indivisibility, about which there would be little argument, there is considerable disagreement as to the likely shape of the long-run cost curve. On the one hand there are

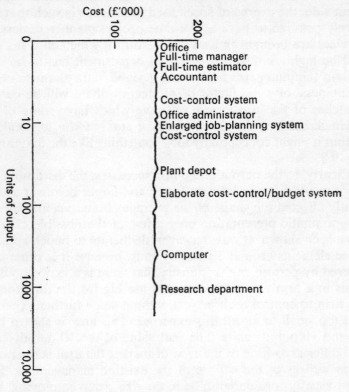

FIG. 9.8. Possible humps in long-run average cost curves

economies of scale *per se* which would tend to a falling cost curve, and on the other hand there is supposedly one final indivisibility which is entrepreneurial ability (in which one might include not only the decision-making process but also the organisational framework) and also a possibility of rising factor costs.

Many studies of manufacturing industries have tried to find evidence for the shape of the long-run cost curve,[7, 18] but their findings are not consistent and not generally applicable to construction.

Hague (1969)[9] observes that such statistical evidence as there is suggests that in many firms the long-run cost curve does not turn up to the right but is more L-shaped, falling fast at first as fixed costs are spread over more and more output and then falling slowly or remaining more or less constant. He notes that statistical research has concentrated on rather large firms and says that it could be that in industries where small firms predominate, the long-run average cost curve slopes sharply up to the right. He goes on to say:

One reason why the long-run average cost curve slopes downwards is likely to be that there is technical progress. The firm can produce more cheaply as time goes on because its production methods become more efficient. This means that, strictly speaking, the curve that statisticians identify from looking at data over a period of time may not be a single curve but a composite one. For example, suppose that the firm in Fig. 9.9* has experienced two big reductions in production costs during the time in question. It began producing in its present plant with the average cost curve AC_1; later costs fell so that the average cost curve became AC_2; a further fall in costs has meant that it now produces on the curve AC_3.

A statistical study might also show that in the initial situation the firm was producing the output OM with unit costs OC. Later, when the relevant cost curve was AC_2 the output of OM_1 might have been produced at a unit cost of OC_1. Recently the firm may have been observed to produce the output OM_2 at a unit cost of OC_2. It would be possible in a correct sense to join points A, B and C by a long-run cost curve. However, this would be a historical rather than an analytical cost curve. It would not, as the economist's cost curve usually does, show how cost and output were related in a given plant in a given state of technology. Before one draws conclusions about any individual cost curve identified by statisticians it is important to be quite clear whether it refers to one state of technology or to a number of successive states.

*The diagram number has been changed to correspond with those in this book.

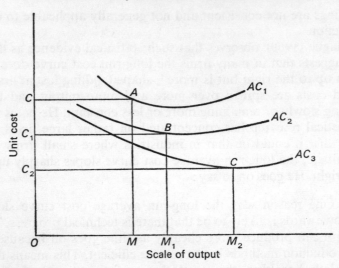

FIG. 9.9. Shift of cost curves with change in technology over time

It is quite possible that it is the case in the construction industry that the large companies have been moving on a decreasing cost curve over time and through different technologies. There were no very large companies before the war, and since the war there have been a number of advances in plant and management techniques. This would account for the increase in size in spite of the problem of controlling a large organisation – even if it is split up into a large number of operating companies.

The advantages of being large are many, even once all the economies of using large units of specialised plant and knowledge have been obtained. First, a large company has advantages on the financial side. Its reserves for risk do not have to increase in proportion to its turnover as, with an increasing number of projects, the probability that they will all show losses together decreases. Another aspect of the decreasing risk with an increase in size is that the large firm can afford to take larger risks with a possible reward of higher profits on average. Moreover, if a company wishes to obtain finance, its size gives it direct access to the capital market and its very size gives confidence to investors.

One factor which is important in contracting is that the large company is sufficiently big to be able to obtain all the technical and managerial economies of scale in a number of markets, e.g. housing and roads, at the same time, thus allowing it to gain the advantages of specialisation and of the risk-spreading of diversification.

On the employment side too, there are great advantages in being able to offer good career prospects for management, and in the purchase of materials size may give the large firm bargaining advantages, not only in price but also in delivery dates and service.

Much of the traditional economic analysis assumes that the long-run average cost curve of the firm will not go on decreasing or even stay at a constant level, but eventually must turn up. One reason why the firm may face a rising long-run average cost curve is that some inputs cannot be increased except at a higher price. This raises all sorts of questions about the level of competition which are discussed in Chapter 12. However, it is clear that if the firm has a large share of the market, the prices of its inputs could rise quite steeply. Sand and gravel, for example, may have to come from considerably further afield or from pits more expensive to operate if the demands are large. On the other hand it may be that the ability to purchase supplies of materials in bulk might offset any increase due to other factors.

A firm operating in a limited geographical area may well find that substantially to increase its turnover means extending its catchment area, and hence its costs of transport and supervision as travelling time increases. Similarly, the geographical spread of demand for projects may not coincide with the availability of manpower so that the price of labour may rise with expansion in turnover, either because of increased transport costs or because of the bargaining power of the operatives.

Another reason put forward for eventually increasing long-run average costs is the indivisible nature of 'entrepreneurial ability' – that the decision-making process gets clogged. Williamson (1967)[10] has applied organisation theory to this problem. He says:

> For any given span of control (together with a specification of the state of technology, internal experience, etc.) an irreducible minimum degree of control loss results from the

simple serial reproduction distortion that occurs in communicating across successive hierarchical levels. If in addition goals differ between hierarchical levels, the loss of control can be extensive.

This conclusion immediately brings to mind Bishop's (1971)[11] simulation of projects in which he found that the reduction in the number of stages of a project from 12 to 10 'is roughly equivalent to that obtained by improving control of activities from relatively coarse to fine'. Certainly, research to follow up the leads of Bishop's work into the management of the whole firm would appear to be a potentially fruitful field. There may be many firms which are on a long-run increasing cost curve. Only detailed analysis of firms in the field would show whether this was the reason why they are at their existing size. There are, however, some firms in the United Kingdom which do not yet appear to have reached the point of increasing long-run average cost. Many of the largest firms (and the largest firms in the United Kingdom are among the largest in the world) have been expanding their turnover so that even with an adjustment for inflation they are still becoming larger. They may still be gaining some additional advantages from their size, but these are likely to be small. They seem to have been able to overcome the supposed fixity of entrepreneurial ability.

PROBLEM OF GROWTH OVER TIME

Some reference has already been made to the problem of assessing costs over time when technology has changed (see quotation from Hague (1969)[9] above). In addition, in a consideration of short-run costs it was found that there were costs of changing from one level of output and, in the instance quoted, particularly from one level of employment to another and that these might not be the same when output was rising as when output was falling, i.e. the cost curves worked in one direction but were not reversible.

The problem of time and of rate of growth over time affects a great many other relationships between output and cost. First, there are advantages, not only in being large as already discussed, but also in *getting* large. It is generally easier to introduce technological change if, at least for the pilot project using the new process, skills can be brought in from outside without detriment to the employment of those already in the organisation. For a factory process it is easier to open a factory using new methods and a reduced *proportion* of manpower if the growth of the firm is such that the total men employed need not be reduced, thus leading to poor morale. Similarly, a growing company – even more obviously than a large company – will be able to attract high-calibre staff at a relatively favourable price.

There are corresponding difficulties and costs for a company which is shrinking in size: the Redundancy Payments Act mentioned earlier is just one of the many costs. However, the adjustments which must take place in the organisation of the firm as it grows and the problems of adjustment mean that there is probably a maximum rate over time at which growth can take place or, to put it in theoretical terms, there is a maximum rate at which the factors fixed in the short term can be made variable. In theory, it might be possible to change from a firm of £10,000 turnover to £10 million turnover in the space of time in which factors fixed in the short run could be varied. In practice, it seems necessary to go relatively slowly through the in-between stages (partly because of the problem of finding work) because of the other factors not thought to be fixed, which are discovered to be fixed in practice. One reason, for example, why a firm may find it difficult to grow at a fast rate is that working capital will not be available, i.e. it is in danger of over-trading. If it is able to obtain capital, it may have to pay a higher rate of interest. This is not a cost in the usual sense if the willingness of banks and others to finance the firm is determined more by the *rate* at which they are willing to increase lending than by the absolute level of lending.

It is suggested therefore that there will be a cost curve, which is valid for a planning period, which rises as output is increased beyond a certain level because of the difficulty of absorption of the additional resources needed, particularly in terms of human relationships and appropriate organisational adjustments, and also possibly in the difficulty of obtaining the resources of working capital. If the latter is obtained by a bank loan, for example, its provision will be dependent on satisfactory progress at recent rates of growth, thus precluding a very rapid increase in this rate. Fig. 9.10 shows such a series of curves, on the assumption that the long-run cost curve *AB* is declining slightly over a long range of output and that management, labour, plant and equipment, etc., can be obtained in as large quantities as required. Each cost curve is considered to be relevant to a year, but the planning period is assumed to be longer

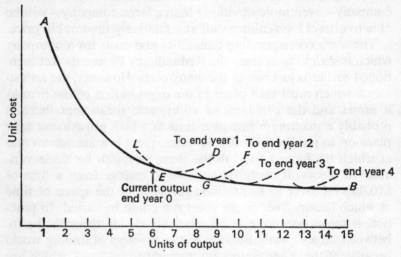

FIG. 9.10. Average cost curves for each of a series of years, assuming two-year planning periods

– say two years. Thus at the end of year 1 plans can be made of increasing output in two years' time to 7 units, i.e. to *E*. However, if output is pushed beyond *E* in this period, costs will rise substantially along *ED*. Assuming that output will be satisfactorily extended to *E* at the end of year 1, at the end of year 0 plans can be made for year 2 for which the effective cost curve (by the end of year 1) will be *EGF*. However, if plans are not made two years in advance, the cost curve for year 2 would probably turn up before point *G*. The increase in output possible in each succeeding period will not always be constant because, as indicated by Fig. 9.8 for example, the problems will be different at each stage.

These period cost curves can be regarded as special cases of short-run cost curves over time. Although in the exposition above it has been assumed that the firm is aiming at growth, in fact it is equally true that if it falls behind its planned expansion it is also likely to experience an increase in costs, as shown by the U shape of the curve, for example *LED*.

There is some support for this theoretical concept from data obtained from firms. The Ashridge study (Lea *et al.*, 1972)[2] found that: 'Firms mostly considered that a growth in real terms of about 10 per cent per annum was the maximum desirable. There was evidence of profits falling in some of the firms when growth was too rapid. The limiting factors mentioned were professional staff and site agents – rarely labour.'

It is quite frequent in discussions with senior management in the industry that their plans are expressed in terms of a desirable rate of growth in output. Some had grown faster than planned and acknowledge that they were unable to consolidate sufficiently. As has been mentioned earlier, it is not easy in the construction industry, by reason of the uncertainties of the tendering situation, to regulate work load. Moreover, once a firm has acquired the work and recruited the necessary staff, it is loath to dismiss it again and revert to the planned growth rate. This staff tends to become the new norm, and planned growth is superimposed on the new higher norm. If this is correct, it would account for the belief among observers of the industry that many of the failures are basically due to lack of working capital.

SUPPLY CURVE OF THE FIRM

The output which the firm is prepared to supply at any price is shown by the marginal cost curve so long as this lies above the average cost curve. This must be so, for if the firm is not covering the additional cost of producing another unit of output, then it would be better not to produce it. When the marginal cost curve lies between the average total cost curve and the average variable cost curve the firm will still find it worth while to produce near the output shown by the marginal curve. This is because in this area – small for most contracting firms because of the low level of fixed costs – it is covering the additional costs of the project even though it is not making its full contribution to head office overheads. If the marginal cost curve is below the average variable cost curve, the firm should not produce at all. In all this analysis the relevant marginal and average cost curves are those related to whatever time period is under consideration. Thus in the short run the supply curve of the firm will slope upwards to the right fairly steeply. In the long run the supply curve may be relatively constant for quite large ranges of output, although, assuming unchanged technologies, it would probably eventually turn up.

10 Market Supply Curves

While it is a truism that the supply curve of the market is made up of the total of what the firms in that market are able to supply at various prices, the variability of firms complicates the summation of individual supply curves. Moreover, other factors, which could be ignored for the firm having a relatively small share of the market, may dominate the market supply curve, thus making the total market supply curve different from the sum of the individual firms' supply curves. These problems are discussed below and the conclusion for the supply curves of the firm and of the market are summarised in Table 10.1.

EFFICIENCY OF FIRMS

If firms were all of equal efficiency, there were no changes in price of factors of production with changes in output, and firms were all aiming to maximise profits, the supply curve of the market would be the same shape as the supply curve of the individual firm (although with different values of output on the horizontal axis). The position is illustrated in Fig. 10.1, where AB is both the supply curve of the individual firm, using the firm scale of output, and of the market, using the market scale of output and assuming that there are 100 firms operating in this market.

If, however, the firms are different in efficiency owing to differences in entrepreneurs (the other assumptions remaining the same), the most inefficient producer will have the highest average cost curve – and it will be just covered by price, otherwise he will leave the industry – and the other producers will have lower average cost curves which will be more than covered by price so that they make higher profits as a reward for their superior entrepreneurial ability. These profits may or may not

TABLE 10.1
Possible Variants in the Supply Curves

INDIVIDUAL FIRMS	Short run for firm	Long run for firm	Long run for firm and market	No time restrictions
1. Average costs:				
(a) increasing	√	√	√	–
(b) constant	–	√	√	–
(c) decreasing	–	√	√	–
2. Importance of profit motive:				
(a) firms maximise profits	√	√	√	–
(b) firms do not maximise profits	–	√	√	–
3. Time-span:				
(a) short run – some factors fixed	√	–	–	–
(b) long run – no factors fixed	–	√	√	–
(c) unlimited amount of growth possible	–	–	–	√
MARKET				
4. Degree of homogeneity:				
(a) all firms equal efficiency	√	√	√	–
(b) firms not equal efficiency	√	√	√	–
5. Extent of shortage of factors of production:				
(a) some factors in short supply	√	√	√	–
(b) no factors in short supply	–	√	√	–
6. Prices of factors of production:				
(a) increasing with increase in demand	√	√	√	–
(b) constant with increase in demand	√	√	√	–
(c) decreasing with increase in demand	–	√	√	–
7. Number of firms:				
(a) fixed	√	√	–	–
(b) not fixed, i.e. free entry and exit	–	√	√	–

be higher than normal profit, i.e. that just sufficient to keep them in the industry. Whether or not the market cost curve with variably efficient producers will be higher or lower than that with homogeneous producers cannot be known, since the efficiency of the homogeneous producers relative to the heterogeneous ones is not known.

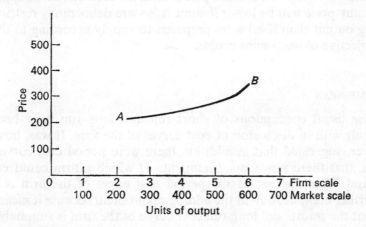

Fig. 10.1. Supply curve of firm and market on assumption of identical cost curves of firms

In fact it is clear that in the construction industry all entrepreneurs are not equally efficient and therefore that some producers have lower costs than others and may earn profits rather higher than those which would be just enough to keep them in the industry.

The general principle of the summation of the cost curves of the individual firms to obtain the supply curve of the market may be applied for the short run or for the long run.

IMPORTANCE OF PROFIT OBJECTIVE

It was suggested under the consideration of the objectives of the firm that firms might not all maximise profits or wish to do so. In this case the effective supply curves of the firms which have to be summed are not the theoretical cost curves showing how much they can economically produce at a given price, but the effective cost curves showing how much they are actually *prepared* to produce at a given price. For example, it may be that family firms wish to limit the size of the firm to that which can be managed by the family, or that after a certain amount of profit the entrepreneur values leisure more than profits. In both these cases their supply curve will be different from their marginal cost curve, with a cut-off point more like that in manufacturing industry due to fixed plant. Thus the total effective supply at any price will be lower if some firms are deliberately restricting output than if all were prepared to supply according to the objective of maximum profits.

TIME-SPAN

The usual conceptions of short run and long run have been dealt with in discussion of cost curves of the firm. It was, however, suggested that in addition there were period cost curves, i.e. that there was a maximum rate at which a firm could expand. This concept of the period cost curve of the firm is a further complication in the adding-up problem because it means that the traditional long-run cost curve of the firm is summable for all firms only over a period of time much longer than normally considered.

SHORTAGE AND PRICE OF FACTORS OF PRODUCTION

It is quite possible that the market will be unable to obtain certain factors of production in the quantities required: for example, there simply may not be enough of a certain type of engineer to manage a large increase in the volume of a type of specialised project; there may not be enough carpenters in a certain area to enable the traditional housebuilding programme to be, say, doubled; there may not be enough copper pipe to allow a substantial increase in the rate of output of domestic central heating systems. Some of these may create a definite limit for a period of time to the output within the market, but it will probably at the same time create a change in the cost curve of the market, because the increased demand for a particular commodity will tend to raise its price to a new equilibrium balancing its demand and supply.

Other shortages of factors of production may be able to be overcome in physical terms, but again only by an increase in the cost curve of the market. It may be possible to attract specialist engineers from abroad; to pay overtime to carpenters or provide transport and additional earnings to bring them from other areas; to import copper pipe from abroad. Some of these methods of overcoming the shortage will provide equally efficient resources at a higher price, others may provide less efficient resources at the same price, and others again less efficient resources at a higher price. In each case the effect is to raise the cost curve of the market.

In the long run the industries (or other institutions) producing the factors of production will react to the shift in the demand curve for their product and will be able to expand output. It will depend on the cost curves for the factors of production whether the long-run price will be higher than, the same as or lower than that at lower outputs.

There will be no increase in the cost of factors of production (or a shortage of supply) if an individual firm alone expands its output, so long as its market share is imperceptible. However, if there are a few firms in a market, any one firm may be affected by a shortage of factors of production. In this connection it should, however, be pointed out that any market for the products of the construction industry may be served by factor markets which cover a number of different markets, e.g. steel, so that, except in specific cases, of which some examples have been suggested above, the individual firm and the individual market may have a relatively small share of the total demand of factors of production.

ENTRY TO AND EXIT FROM THE MARKET

One of the conditions of equilibrium in the industry is that there is no incentive for firms to enter or leave the industry.

A firm will in the long run leave the industry if it is not making normal profits, i.e. if it is not covering the rate of return the firm could attract on its capital elsewhere, plus remuneration for its directors equivalent to that which they could earn elsewhere, adjusted for the entrepreneurs who are content to accept a lower rate of return on themselves and their capital because they value other advantages more highly. These entrepreneurs may or may not be maximising profits.

Firms will wish to enter the market if they think they can make at least normal profits in the market, either because they think they are more efficient than the least efficient producer, or because the ruling price is higher than the average cost of the least efficient producer – owing, for example, to a shift in the demand curve. The latter situation may obtain, even if the long-run cost curve of the existing firms is constant or decreasing, if the rate at which the existing firms can grow is lower than the required increase in demand in the time period necessary for new firms to enter the market.

In the long run free entry to and exit from the market will tend to lead to a situation where all firms in the market are producing at minimum average cost so that the long-run market supply curve may be horizontal or rising slightly if new firms are less efficient.

DISCUSSION AND ASSESSMENT OF FACTORS AFFECTING THE MARKET SUPPLY CURVE

It will be seen from Table 10.1 that in each period considered the possible combinations of each of the variants is very great: for example, in the long run for the firm it is 144.* Even if some of the variants are assumed to be constant, for example the average costs, it still leaves a number so large that it is neither feasible nor helpful to construct a model for each situation. Some general observations may, however, be made.

The only situation in which factors not directly considered in the cost curve of the individual firm are likely to lead to a decrease in the long-run supply curve of the market is that in

---

*i.e. 3 possible average costs, for the firm combined with
    2 possible attitudes to profits
    1 time-span
together with, for the market,
    2 possibilities of homogeneity of firms
    2 possibilities of shortage of factors of production
    3 possible prices of factors of production
and 2 possibilities of the number of firms, i.e.

$$3 \times 2 \times 1 \times 2 \times 2 \times 3 \times 2 = 144.$$

which factors of production have a decreasing cost curve, i.e. 6(c) in Table 10.1. Although this may be the case for one or two inputs of the construction market, it is unlikely to be true over the whole range of inputs. Therefore, having regard to the fact that at any given level of knowledge the long-run average cost curve of the individual firm is likely to be decreasing at best almost insignificantly, it is virtually ruled out that the long-run supply curve of the market at any given time is other than rising, although over a long period of time with different technologies it could slope downwards (See Chapter 9).

The short-run supply curve of the market will also be rising and will, as in the case of the individual firms, be considerably steeper than the long-run supply curve.

11 Equilibrium in Various Market Situations

It was shown at the beginning of Chapter 9 how the costs of the individual large contract obtained at a single point in time but with work spread over a long period are relevant to the usual cost curves of economic analysis which represent the answer to the question: If the output of the firm were higher or lower than a given level, what would be the effect on costs? The remainder of the chapter was devoted to a detailed consideration of this question.

By an analysis almost identical to that for costs, the revenue obtained from individual projects may be transformed into revenue over time and then consideration be given to the likely difference in revenue at a point in time if the output had been larger or smaller than a given level. This is the demand curve of the firm. It is dependent on the one hand on the demand curve of the industry or market under consideration and, on the other hand, on the position of the individual firm in the market in question. The first was discussed in the demand section of this book, i.e. Chapters 4–7. The second requires a preliminary general investigation of the various theoretical types of market situation, because the demand curve of the individual firm in some conditions, notably oligopoly and discriminating monopoly, cannot be understood without reference to the analysis of both demand and supply. This is the subject of the present chapter. In Chapter 12 consideration is given to the place of the construction firm in various markets on the theoretical range from perfect competition to monopoly.

Before embarking on the analysis of cost and revenue in various market situations, it is advisable first to pause and consider the relationship of average revenue, which is the demand curve facing the firm or the industry, to total revenue and marginal revenue, both of which concepts are necessary for the analysis following.

AVERAGE, TOTAL AND MARGINAL REVENUE

The demand curve is the average revenue curve of the firm or the industry as the case may be. From it the total revenue and thence the marginal revenue curve may be derived. Alternatively, just as in the case of costs, the analysis may commence with the total revenue of the firm and the average revenue be derived from it by the slope of the cord and the marginal revenue by the slope of the tangent. The pairs of diagrams in Fig. 11.1A–E show the relationship between these in varying demand circumstances.

In Fig. 11.1A, elasticity of demand is less than 1, i.e. following the analysis in Chapter 4, the total amount spent on the commodity decreases and, as elasticity is constant, the total revenue curve is a straight line. Clearly, the marginal revenue must be constant and negative because the tangent to the falling revenue curve is constant and of negative slope. The market demand for the output of construction is usually inelastic.

Fig. 11.1B shows elasticity of demand equal to unity. This means that the total amount spent on the commodity is constant and the average revenue curve is a rectangular hyperbola. Marginal revenue is nil and constant.

Fig. 11.1C shows elasticity of demand greater than 1 and constant. The total revenue curve is a rising straight line, the average revenue is a rather flat curve and marginal revenue is constant and positive.

Fig. 11.1D shows the situation where the elasticity of demand is infinite. This is of interest because it represents the position of the demand curve of the firm under perfect competition. Average revenue equals marginal revenue and the total curve is a straight line with a slope of 1.

Lastly, in Fig. 11.1E the elasticity of demand is first greater than 1, then less than 1. The demand curve, i.e. the average revenue curve, is shown in this diagram as a straight line falling to the right and the marginal revenue curve similarly decreases to the right. From this diagram it can be seen that the average revenue curve is the slope of the cord of the total curve and the marginal revenue curve the slope of the tangent. When marginal revenue is nil, the total is at its highest point.

Total

Average and Marginal

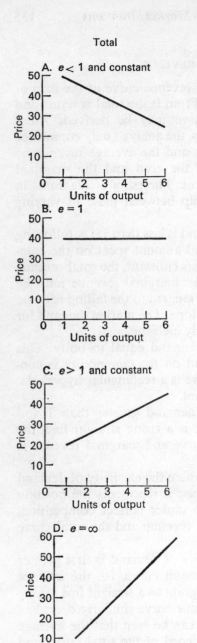

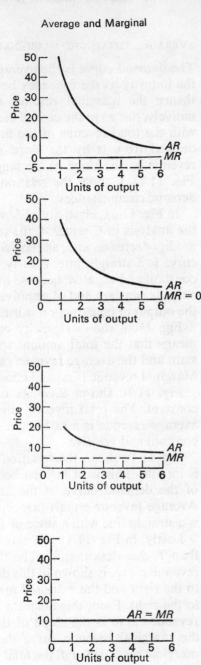

A. *e* < 1 and constant

B. *e* = 1

C. *e* > 1 and constant

D. *e* = ∞

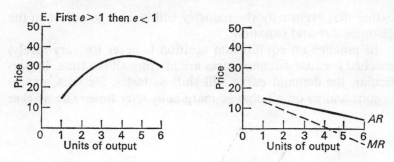

FIG. 11.1. Total, average and marginal revenue curves

MARKET EQUILIBRIUM

Equilibrium exists in the market when:

(*a*) the price is such that demand and supply are equal at that price;

(*b*) there is no incentive for firms to move out of or into the market;

(*c*) there is no incentive for producers to change their output, method of production or price.

In all markets the price at which goods will be sold is that which balances the amount on offer with that demanded. It was found in Chapters 4–6 that the demand curve for construction will have varying elasticities depending, *inter alia*, on the type of construction under consideration, and in Chapter 10 the short-run supply curve was found to slope upwards to the right and the long-run supply curve to be gently upward-sloping or even horizontal. Over a long term in which technical knowledge is not fixed, there may well be a long-run cost curve for the industry which decreases over time. Thus, while in the short run a shift in the demand curve for construction may well cause a rise in price, in the long run the industry may be able to meet demand with little or no increase in costs. This is illustrated in Fig. 11.2, in which D_1 is the demand curve in period 1 and D_2 is the demand curve for period 2 shifted upwards, as a result, for instance, of a rise in real incomes. S_1 is the short-run supply curve which shows that in the short-term the new demand will be met only at a higher price. S_2 is the long-run supply curve more or less constant over a large range of output, indicating that eventually the industry will be able to adjust to the changed demand situation.

In practice an equilibrium position is never (or very rarely) reached because circumstances are altering all the time. In particular, the demand curve will shift as tastes, incomes, expectations and so on all change marginally over time. The market

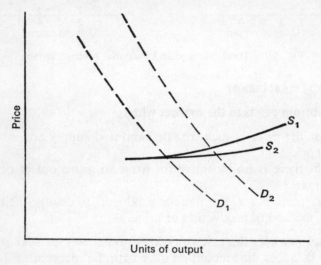

FIG. 11.2. Long-run and short-run equilibria

will, however, always be attempting to move towards an equilibrium position. To understand the changes in the market supply position, it is necessary to investigate the various possible relationships of the firms in the market to each other and to the total market situation.

Economic theory distinguishes a number of market types with perfect competition at one extreme and monopoly at the other extreme. In between is an infinite range of imperfect competition. On the buying side too there is a range of possibilities from one buyer – monopsony – to an infinite number of buyers.

PERFECT COMPETITION

The main characteristics of a perfectly competitive market are:

1. Homogeneous product, that is, each producer must be selling a product which is indistinguishable from those of other producers.

2. Large number of firms so that each firm produces an insignificant proportion of total output.

3. Free entry to the market.

4. Perfect knowledge of what everyone else is selling and at what price.

Similar criteria exist on the purchaser's side – in particular that there are so many buyers that each one purchases an insignificant proportion of total output.

The existence of all these conditions together leads to a condition of perfect competition – sometimes approached, for example, in a grain market, but never actually in practice achieved. Sometimes a rather more realistic model of pure competition is used embodying criteria 1–3 but dropping that of perfect knowledge.

In perfect competition in equilibrium all firms will have the same costs. This does not mean that all firms are identical, but simply that if one firm has, say, a more efficient manager than others, then the price which he will be able to charge for his services will be such that he takes all the benefit he gives the firm with his superior efficiency. If he were not paid this amount, under competitive conditions he could move to another firm where he would be.

In Fig. 11.3A, SL_1 and SS respectively are the long-term and short-term supply curves of the market assuming that no new firms enter the market. They have the same shape as the relevant part of the marginal cost curves of the firm in Fig. 11.3B. In Fig. 11.3A D_1 is the demand curve. It cuts the supply curves at A so that output is OB and price OP_1.

Assume then that there is a shift in the demand curve to D_2 in Fig. 11.3A. The short-run equilibrium will be at C with price P_2. In the long term, if there were no possibility of other firms entering the industry, equilibrium would be at E with price P_3.

The position of the firm is shown in Fig. 11.3B. ACS and

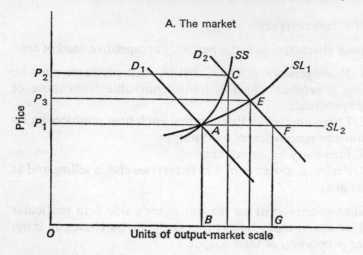

A. The market

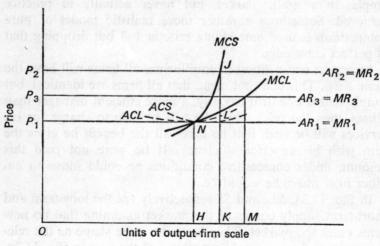

B. The firm

FIG. 11.3. Perfect competition

ACL are the short and long-run average cost curves and MCS and MCL the marginal cost curves of the firm. AR_1 is the average revenue curve at the market equilibrium price P_1. This is the price which the individual firm obtains no matter how much it produces. The output of this one firm is, according to the definition of perfect competition, such a small fraction of the market's output that even a large change in the output of this firm affects the total output of the market to only an infinitesimal degree. If the firm sells at a price below this ruling price, since there is perfect knowledge, it would be able to sell all its output but its average costs would be greater than average revenue and it would therefore go out of business. If it quoted a price above the ruling price level, it would sell nothing because, again assuming perfect knowledge, every buyer would go elsewhere. As the average revenue is constant, it is equal to marginal revenue so that AR_1 is both the average and the marginal revenue curve. The optimum position for any firm is always that at which its marginal revenue equals its marginal cost. This must be so because, if the revenue from an additional unit of output were greater than the cost of producing that additional output, then it would pay to go on expanding output until there was no advantage in further expansion, i.e. so that marginal revenue was equal to the marginal cost of its production. Similarly, if the revenue from an additional unit of output is less than the marginal cost of its production, then the firm would be better off contracting production until it is no longer making a loss on the last unit.

Thus at price P_1 the optimum position for the firm is at the output at which the marginal revenue curve MR_1 cuts the marginal cost curves MCS and MCL, i.e. at N where output will be OH. The average cost and average revenue at this point are also equal, so that the firm will earn only normal profits. When the market demand curve shifts, the new short-run price level ruling in the market becomes P_2. The new average and marginal revenue curves of the firm become AR_2 and MR_2. The optimum output becomes OK, i.e. that output at which the marginal revenue curve MR_2 cuts the marginal cost curve MCS at J. At this output the average revenue or price is KJ and the average cost KL, so that the firm is making a supernormal profit of JL on each unit of output. In the longer term but with the number of firms still fixed the price becomes P_3 and output rises to OM. The firm still has a supernormal profit.

If new firms can enter the industry, they will do so because they will be attracted by the supernormal profits. If they can obtain factors of production at the same prices, they will enter until they shift the long-run supply curve to SL_2 in Fig. 11.3A. Equilibrium will then be at F with price P_1 as before and output OG. The output of the firm will revert to its original level at output OH in Fig. 11.3B with no supernormal profit. The increase in the output of the market as a whole would then be made up entirely by the output of the new firms entering the market.

MONOPOLY

At the other extreme of market conditions is monopoly, i.e. where there is one producer and seller. In these circumstances the average revenue curve of the monopolist is the same as the demand curve of the industry, so that the average price received per unit of output falls as more output is put on the market. When average revenue is falling, marginal revenue is below average revenue and falling faster. Thus in Fig. 11.4, if AR is the market demand curve and the average revenue curve of the monopolist, then MR is the marginal revenue curve. SL is

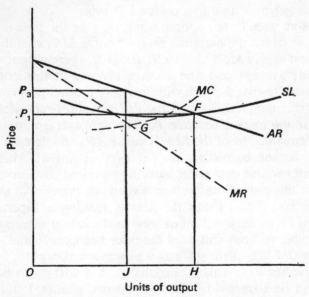

FIG. 11.4. Monopoly: the market and the firm

the long-run cost curve which would approximate to the supply curve of the industry under competitive conditions, although it might not be the same. On the one hand it might be lower because the monopolist might be able to obtain economies of scale by unifying production and, on the other hand, it might be higher as the monopolist might require a more bureaucratic organisation and, for example, indulge in a large industry advertising campaign. The marginal cost curve is MC. The price under competitive conditions would be determined by where the demand curve cuts the supply curve, i.e. at F with price P_1 and output OH. In the case of the monopoly firm, however, the position of maximum profit would be obtained where the marginal cost curve cuts the marginal revenue curve, i.e. at G. Price would be P_3 for output OJ, i.e. a higher price and a lower output than that under conditions of competition.

It is possible for a situation of monopoly to be one of equilibrium according to the three conditions listed above. The price is one which equates demand and supply – although the supply is entirely determined by the one producer and there may well be no incentive for the producer to change his output, method of production or price. The real question arises on whether there is incentive for firms to move out of or into the market. Situations do arise in which the monopoly is based on technical economies of scale. If the cheapest way of producing the product is on a scale which is as great as the whole industry, there would be no incentive for any firm to enter the industry for it could not compete at an output lower than that of the whole industry. (Indeed, it would be theoretically feasible that the lowest cost of the optimum scale of production was achieved at outputs greater than the industry output. In this case the cost curve could be falling, and if it were steeper than the demand curve there would be no equilibrium position.) In other cases, however, the monopolist is being constantly threatened by new entrants and he may have to limit the amount of monopoly profit he makes in order to discourage new entrants. In practice he may find it desirable to limit profits and behave in a way similar to the competitive situation so that he does not break any anti-monopoly law or lead to a situation in which legislation would be considered desirable.

One peculiar form of monopolistic situation must be mentioned, namely that of discriminating monopoly. This arises when there is no possibility of reselling the product from one buyer to another. This enables the monopolist to split up his markets and sell at a higher price in markets where demand is relatively inelastic and at a lower price in markets where demand is elastic, thus maximising profits in each market. The sum of the profits will be greater than the profit obtained by treating the market as one. The classic example of this practice is that of the doctors who charge higher fees to rich patients than to poor ones. A limited form of discriminating monopoly may also exist when the product of the market may be resold but where the resale value is for some reason lower than the value at the point of first sale. The latter case has some relevance to construction, as will be seen later.

OTHER FORMS OF IMPERFECT COMPETITION

In fact most industries and markets lie somewhere in between perfect competition and monopoly. It will be convenient to consider these in two main sectors of the number of firms and the extent to which products are differentiated.

Oligopoly

A market in which there are few producers and in which, therefore, the actions of the individual firm do have an effect on the overall market is known as a situation of oligopoly, i.e. a few producers, just as monopoly denotes one producer. Each of the firms in a position of oligopoly will have a share of the total market. Assuming the market average cost curve is the same for oligopoly as for monopoly, the optimum price, i.e. that which maximises profits, at which they would sell their products would be the same as that at which the monopolist would sell, as this is the price which maximises profit in the market as a whole and would therefore maximise the size of the share of each oligopolist. However, if one or more of the oligopolists decided to cut price to obtain a larger share of the market, because there were so few producers, his action would be obvious and would be seen as a threat to the market share of the others. They would therefore tend to cut their prices by the same amount or more. This process could be continued until the oligopolists had so reduced their prices that they were earning only normal profit, and in this case their output would be the same as that under perfect competition. The actual price level could be anywhere in between these two extremes.

It is interesting that, in a position of oligopoly, there might well be no reaction from competitors to a rise in price. They would not see this as a threat to their positions. Thus the demand curve facing the oligopolist may well be kinked, as shown in Fig. 11.5. Assume the ruling price is that at point *B* on the

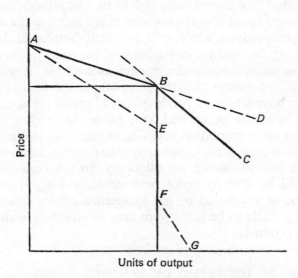

FIG. 11.5. Oligopoly: kinked demand curve

demand curve *AD*. Then above that price, if the oligopolist increases price this will not induce his competitors to act similarly and he moves along the curve *AB* – which is essentially his share of the market demand curve. If, however, he reduces price, the other producers will also reduce price so that his output will not increase as much as if he could do this without retaliation and move downwards along his share of the market demand curve from *B* to *D*. In fact he will find himself on the line *BC*. His average revenue curve will therefore be *ABC*. The corresponding marginal revenue curve is the broken line *AEFG*. If his marginal cost curve passes between *E* and *F*, then the entrepreneur will not move from his initial position at *B*. Not until his marginal costs are as low as or lower than F would it pay him to reduce price. For this reason, in a situation of oligopoly, there is a strong incentive for all the firms to form a tacit or overt agreement not to enter into a price war. Competition may tend to take other forms, such as that of product differentiation.

Product Differentiation

In a market in which there are many firms, each producing a product slightly different from that of its competitors, each firm will be faced by an average revenue curve showing the demand for its own products which will be nearly horizontal, i.e. near to perfectly competitive conditions, if its own products have very close substitutes in the market as a whole. It will slope the more, the greater the degree to which the firm is able to convince buyers that its products have special features. These features, it should be noticed, may be in the product itself, in its wrappings, presentation, location of sales points, etc.

This product differentiation may also occur in markets where there are few producers, i.e. oligopoly. In this case the oligopolist will be able to make price changes without so much likelihood of retaliation by his competitors. Price competition, at least, is likely to be less severe than in oligopoly with homogeneous products.

MEASURES OF THE EXTENT OF MONOPOLY POWER

It will be noted from the above discussion of various market situations that the more the individual producer is able, through product differentiation or simply by being one of a few in the market, to keep to himself a piece of that market, the greater the slope of his average revenue curve (assuming that the market demand curves have equal elasticity). Thus a measure of the degree of monopoly power is the difference between the price which the firm charges and its marginal cost. In perfect competition, marginal cost is equal to price. In monopoly it is considerably less than price. This measure has disadvantages, however, since it is dependent not only on the market form, but also on the slope of the industry demand curve. Another measure of the degree of monopoly is the extent of supernormal profits earned by firms in the market. Clearly, both measures have value, but the overall situation must be examined before a judgement is made.

IMPORTANCE OF FREEDOM OF ENTRY

So long as there are no barriers to the entry of firms into the market, a substantial degree of monopoly power cannot long be maintained. However, barriers may be technological, i.e. the scale of production may be such that no small company can enter the market or the market is not large enough to support more than a few firms. If there are no such technological barriers to entry, it is possible that the existing firms in the market may not exercise their full monopoly power for fear of attracting new entrants to the industry. There is usually some initial non-recurring cost of entering a new market in the form of market research and other investment, and if the existing firms keep their prices so low that the supernormal profits they earn are small, the attraction to outsiders may not outweigh the initial costs of entry.

OBJECTIVES OTHER THAN PROFIT MAXIMISATION

The effect of assumptions other than that the entrepreneur wishes to maximise profits must be considered. First, the situation of perfect competition will be examined. In this situation each firm is producing at the lowest part of its average cost curve and making only normal profit. If the entrepreneur wished to limit or increase the output of the firm, he would move either back and upwards or forward and upwards on his average cost curve, which, with a constant average revenue curve, means that his profits would be reduced below the normal level. If, on the other hand, he continues to obtain normal profits, then the secondary goal of revenue maximisation implies the same output, because in perfect competition with homogeneous products, average revenue equals marginal revenue equals average cost equals marginal cost. Thus if he wishes to maximise profits he produces the output at which marginal revenue equals marginal cost, which is the same output as that for revenue maximisation with normal profit, i.e. average revenue equals average cost.

In conditions of monopoly the entrepreneur is able to restrict output so that he earns less than maximum profit but his profit is still greater than or equal to normal. If he wishes to earn normal profit and maximise revenue he will extend his output until his average costs (including normal profit) equal his average revenue. Thus in Fig. 11.4, if the entrepreneur did not wish to earn more than normal profit but wished to maximise revenue, he could move from the profit-maximisation output of *OJ* to the revenue-maximisation output of *OH*. This is also the output which would be produced in a perfectly competitive market.

12 Demand Curves Facing the Individual Firm

Having defined in Chapter 11 various theoretical types of market situation, it must now be considered to which broad types the construction industry markets belong. First, the extent to which the characteristics of a perfectly competitive market apply to the construction industry will be discussed.

HOMOGENEITY OF PRODUCT

Bearing in mind that the product of the contracting industry is a service, as discussed in Chapter 3, even within the individual construction market that product is not completely homogeneous. Indeed, in all cases of price determination except perhaps open competitive tender, it is in the interests of contractors to convince clients that the service they offer is in some way superior to the service offered by their competitors, in order that the client might choose them to be on the selective tender list, to negotiate a contract or enter into a package-deal arrangement. This may go so far that they in fact carve out a small specialised market for themselves. This is one aspect of the current trend in the industry towards marketing, and indeed, in the post-war period the package deal has been so delineated that it has become a separate market. A more recent example is the growth of the offer of a management service in which the managing contractor takes a fee for the management of the contract, not actually undertaking any of the construction work with his own firm. Other firms offer a complete industrial or commercial service, including finding a site, finance, managing the construction process, the furnishing of the premises and the removal of the client from his old premises. In speculative housing there are many examples of product differentiation, in some of which the product is closely linked in advertising with a trade name. In each of these cases the firm is moving as far as possible away from perfect competition to the imperfectly competitive product-differentiated market.

Attempts at product differentiation normally all cease, however, if and when the project gets to the tendering stage, and this is still the case for a majority of projects as was shown in Table 7.1. At the tender stage it is assumed that all products are homogeneous and competition takes place purely on price.* The contractor, having successfully persuaded the client that his product is better than that of others and got on to the tender list, has then to put in a price on the basis that he must make his service conform to that laid down in the contract documents, and he knows that he cannot afford to provide a superior service since his tender will be judged on price and not normally on a combination of price and service. Since the product becomes homogeneous at least in the eyes of the client and of the contractor at the tendering stage,† this requirement of perfect competition is met.

NUMBER OF FIRMS

Within some of the construction markets as defined earlier, there are so many firms that each produces an insignificant part of the total output. It is most likely to be so when the sub-industry itself is large and when the size of firm is small. An example is general contracting on the small to medium-sized new building work without any complex technical problems. The small market share of any one contractor is also more likely to occur in areas of relatively dense population where the amount of work within a small area is substantial, so that a large volume of work is available to firms in the area without having to incur heavy transport costs. For large contracts the volume of work is often sufficient to justify fairly independent

---

*There are occasionally exceptions to this when a contractor submits a price based on an alternative design or finishing date, and there are cases in which a price other than the lowest is accepted.

†It should be noted that the product may only appear homogeneous *ex ante. Ex post* some contractors will do a better job than others. Indeed, one of the principal drawbacks of open tendering is that the contractor chosen on price alone may fail to do a satisfactory job, sometimes even going bankrupt.

operation of a site, so that transport costs are not excessive and a substantial number of contractors are willing to work nationally or at least regionally to obtain work of this type. In such cases there are sufficient firms to lead to effective competition at the pre-tender stage. This means that the client at this stage has a large choice of contractors from which to select for tendering or negotiation.

In markets which are small, either because they are limited geographically, such as a small market town in an otherwise rural area, or because they are limited by the degree of specialisation, e.g. suspended-ceiling specialists, or both, there may well exist a situation in which there are only a handful of contractors in the market for any particular size and type of job. This is particularly likely to be so in new types of work, such as multi-storey flats or motorways in the immediate post-war period. Clients do not then have a sufficiently large choice of contractors to fulfil the requirements of an adequate number of firms for anything approaching perfect competition.

In a situation of open competition the number of firms who tender is potentially the whole of the market for that type of contract, but many contractors have decided that they will not do work for which selection is simply by open competition; in effect, therefore, they have created another split in markets by method of appointing the contractor. Within this market it is almost a tautology to say that the firms entering constitute all the firms in this market at that time. The extent of competition as far as the number of firms is concerned is the same as the extent of competition in the market as a whole and, as has just been found, this ranges from effective competition to something which may be considerably less.

In cases of selective tendering, however, the number of firms who participate in the process of price determination and hence compete on price is by the very nature of the process deliberately reduced, so that they are less than in that market as a whole. If the recommendations of the Code of Procedure for Selective Tendering by the National Joint Consultative Committee (1969)[1] are followed, the number will range from four to eight and will certainly be so few that the price submitted by anyone will take into consideration the likely actions of his competitors, i.e. it becomes a situation of oligopoly. The ways in which he can, and to some extent does, take his competitors' position into account is dealt with in detail in Chapter 13 on tendering.

If the number of contractors within any one market falls below a certain level, it becomes more feasible to contemplate some sort of agreement to divide the market so that market shares are predetermined, or to fix price levels. In such a case the group of contractors are virtually by concerted action bringing themselves nearer to the extreme case of monopoly. There have been situations in the construction industry where some form of agreement is alleged to have been operated, and there may still be some. Apart from the restrictions of law, however, the durability of such agreements is severely limited by the free entry to the industry and its markets, dealt with below.

Another way in which competition is limited at the tendering stage is by the taking of cover prices by a contractor not wishing to obtain the job but unwilling to tell the client that he would rather not tender. In such a case the contractor asks another contractor who is on the tender list for a price which he can quote which will be above that quoted by the interested contractor. Although all selected contractors may not know which of those on the list have taken a cover price, the fact that at least the one asked will know reduces the effective number of firms. There may be situations, when demand is strong, when most of the prices submitted are cover prices.

It should be pointed out that there is no need to assume collusion in order to have a situation where the contractors divide the market between them. There must, for example, be many situations where, in a relatively small community, if one builder tries to extend his share of the market by reduction of prices and is efficient enough to do so, there will be some form of retaliation from other local builders. This is a classical situation in oligopoly and is illustrated by the kinked demand curve in Fig. 11.5. In order to avoid a price war, builders may in these circumstances refrain from 'poaching' on each other's traditional clients for fear of similar 'poaching' on their own clients. In such a case profits are likely to be above normal. The continuance of this situation is, however, restricted by ease of entry.

If a contractor is chosen by the client, either by a simplified tendering situation or by any other method, then there is clearly only one firm in the process of final price determination and, based on the number of firms only, this would lead to a monopoly position. In fact, as in so many cases, the power of this position is limited by freedom of entry, not in this case entry into the market, but by the power of the client at any time either to stop negotiations with the one chosen contractor and invite other contractors to negotiate, or to commence the whole process of selection again by going out to tender. The monopoly power of the negotiating contractor will be greater, the greater the time and money already invested by the client in these negotiations, and this money value is a fair measure of the maximum monopoly profits which this contractor might earn.

EASE OF ENTRY TO THE INDUSTRY

One of the safeguards for competition within the industry is that there are no formal restrictions on entry. Moreover, at the lower end of the scale of size of firm the difficulties in setting up in business are slight: capital equipment is negligible – perhaps a spade, a wheelbarrow, a ladder; working capital is not needed for materials as it is provided largely by builders' merchants' credit; working capital for the builder's own remuneration or equivalent of wages is barely necessary as the average duration of small jobs may well be about a week and some householders partly finance this by paying for 'materials' in advance.

Once this elementary stage is passed, graduation for the more efficient rather higher up the scale is not difficult, although there may be crisis points in their progress (see Chapter 9 on costs).

As important as, and, in the more specialised and large-scale project markets, probably much more important than movement up the scale from small to large, is sideways movement from operating in one specialist market to another. Most of the large contractors are in any case working in a considerable number of different markets simultaneously, and if they supect that in work of the appropriate size the profits are abnormally high in a particular specialism, they are likely to buy in expertise in management and enter the market. Similarly, a small builder from one town, hearing that the market in a town near by seems to be particularly profitable, may well move in to obtain work there. He will have little to lose compared with the established group within the town. It is suggested therefore that if the situation exists where, because of a small number of firms in a market profits are abnormally high, freedom of entry and relative ease of entry from a separate but similar market will ensure that the low level of competition does not exist for very long, and work in manufacturing industry in the United States (Bain, 1949,[2] and Mann, 1966[3]) strongly supports this contention.

PERFECT KNOWLEDGE

Clearly, however efficient the construction industry grapevine, there is not perfect knowledge among the contractors of what is happening in the market. Indeed, the whole system of price determination in construction, ranging from open tender to negotiation, ensures that perfect knowledge of which firms are interested in the job and what prices firms are prepared to quote does not exist. Even after the contract is awarded, particulars of the price quoted by each competitor are not automatically made available by the client, especially in the private sector. It is perhaps understandable that there may be a wish to withhold data on negotiated contracts. Some of the secrecy as to the list of tenderers before tenders are due helps to prevent collusion and is a case where more perfect knowledge could cause a movement further away from competition. Some other limitations on knowledge, and particularly that on tender prices after the contract has been awarded, increase uncertainty so that work may go to the best assessor of an uncertain situation rather than the most efficient to undertake the work.

Clearly, the market price does not exist in construction in the same way as the concept is applied, say, to a grain market where the conditions are as near to perfect competition as possible. The product of the contracting industry – assembly, transport, management – is much more difficult to quantify and there is no satisfactory unit of measurement to which to apply the price. Even in the ultimate product of the construction industry, namely the building or other construction work, the product is so variable that when a contractor is making a bid he may have no past data on market price. He does not know the ruling market price but is constantly having to guess at it.

Some of the complications of the uncertainty in this and related situations are dealt with in Chapter 13. It is sufficient here to say that on the criterion of perfect knowledge, perfect competition certainly does not exist in construction.

ASSESSMENT OF EXTENT OF COMPETITION

An examination of the extent to which the conditions for perfect competition are found in the construction industry has shown that no statement can be made which is true for all markets, for all methods of choosing the contractor and of price determination. Table 12.1 shows, for each type of market, each way of selecting a contractor and each stage in the selection process, the type of market conditions. Where there are many firms in the market the types range from near-perfect competition to some limited monopoly – limited, that is, by the ability of the client at any time to remove the contractor from that semi-monopolistic position in which he has put him. The term 'partial oligopoly' is used to denote that the situation is one of oligopoly in the sense that the behaviour of the firm at that stage of the process is influenced by its expectations regarding the behaviour of other firms. It is not full oligopoly because each firm in the tender situation does not have such a large share of the market that his output makes a significant contribution to the total. In all cases in the first part of the table in which there are many firms in the market, the extent of the power to make higher than normal profits is tempered firstly by the knowledge that until the contract is actually signed the client can go back to an earlier stage in the process and bring in more competitive firms, and secondly by the fact that the firms want to be selected for other subsequent contracts and therefore must continually sell themselves as good, moderately priced contractors. In the last resort the client can withdraw his project from the market altogether – at least for a time.

In the second part of the table dealing with markets in which there are only a few firms, there is oligopoly or, in negotiation, monopoly. It is of little help to the client to revert to an earlier

TABLE 12.1
Assessment of Type of Market in Contracting

Type of selection	Stage of selection	Number of firms	Product differentiation	Type of market
I. MANY FIRMS IN THE MARKET				
Open tendering	Tender	Many	None	Approaching perfect competition
Selective tendering	Pre-tender	Many	Substantial	Monopolistic competition
	Tender	Few	None	Partial oligopoly without product differentiation
Two-stage tendering	Pre-tender	Many	Substantial	Monopolistic competition
	Tender	Few	None	Partial oligopoly without product differentiation
	Negotiation	One	n.a.	Limited monopoly
Negotiation	Pre-selection	Many	Substantial	Monopolistic competition
	Post-selection	One	n.a.	Limited monopoly
II. FEW FIRMS IN THE MARKET				
Open tendering	Tender	Few	None	Oligopoly without product differentiation
Selective tendering	Pre-tender	Few	Substantial	Oligopoly with product differentiation
	Tender	Few	None	Oligopoly without product differentiation
Two-stage tendering	Pre-tender	Few	Substantial	Oligopoly with product differentiation
	Tender	Few	None	Oligopoly without product differentiation
	Negotiation	One	n.a.	Limited monopoly
Negotiation	Pre-selection	Few	Substantial	Oligopoly with product differentiation
	Post-selection	One	n.a.	Limited monopoly

stage in the tender process because, even though entry is easy, it may take time to attract firms from other markets. However, the ease of entry is probably of sufficient importance to prevent firms charging prices significantly above normal for any length of time. In this situation too the client can withdraw his project, and may well do so if the price seems to be too high.

LEVEL OF PROFIT IN THE INDUSTRY

One measure of the degree of monopoly power is the extent to which the profits in the industry are higher than normal. There is little up-to-date information on this. However, work carried out for the Bolton Committee (Tamari, 1972)[4] showed that in 1964 and 1968, both quite buoyant years for construction, pre-tax profits (before all interest paid) as a percentage of total assets were 9·0 per cent and 8·5 per cent respectively, compared with higher profits in other non-manufacturing industries except for the wholesale industry, and lower or roughly similar profits for manufacturing industries. Thus on this evidence, if there are situations where there is monopoly power in the industry, they must be relatively unimportant compared with the construction industry as a whole.

INFLUENCE OF THE CLIENT

The actions of the client can substantially determine the degree of competition. There is a great variety of client in the construction industry, from the small unsophisticated client building for the only time in his life, to the large client building more or less continuously and with sophisticated professional advice, often his own employees, at his disposal. The first type of client is likely to be numerous, leading to conditions approaching perfect competition among buyers – although they would certainly not have perfect knowledge. The second are likely to be few, with, in some markets, a monopoly of purchasing, i.e. monopsony; an example is the government as a purchaser of motorways.

In view of the fact, however, that almost all construction projects are separately let, and therefore for a given project the client is the monopsonist, the significance of the nature of the client lies in his degree of sophistication and market knowledge, so that if conditions approaching perfect competition do not exist in that market, he can use his knowledge and power to obtain favourable prices from the existing group of suppliers and, if necesary, increase the degree of competition by going outside the existing suppliers to, say, for a large project, international competition or, for a smaller job, one of the national contractors. If the client is a householder in the repair and maintenance field, he may in a sense be a monopolist buyer but he probably has not the knowledge to use his power.

DEMAND CURVE FACING THE CONTRACTING FIRM

As explained in Chapter 11, under conditions of perfect competition the average and marginal revenue curves of any firm are horizontal and identical and are equal to the price in the market. In the case of monopoly and to some extent in all types of market situation other than perfect or pure competition, the average revenue curve slopes downwards, i.e. as output is increased, the average revenue or price received per unit of output decreases. The slope of the average revenue curve for firms in the construction industry must now be considered specifically.

EFFECT OF THE TYPE OF MARKET

The position in the contracting industry is particularly complicated by the fact that, as shown in Table 12.1, there is, except in open tendering, some non-price competition in which virtually all the firms interested in that particular market at a given time participate and that, once the client has made his selection of one or a group of contractors, price determination takes place among this limited group only. In the case of markets in which there are a few firms only, the number of firms engaged in the price-determination process may be all or nearly all those firms in that market, and therefore in this situation the two processes merge. The only difference is that in the pre-tender stage there is advantage in stressing product differentiation to ensure that the firm is chosen for the price-determination stage. This will be unimportant if the firms are so few that the client has little choice but to include all.

In the latter situation, therefore, there is a fairly clear position of oligopoly. The demand curve of each firm will slope downwards to the right because its share of the market is significant and therefore related to the industry demand curve. It was found in Chapters 4–7 that the industry demand curves for construction tend to be fairly inelastic. The demand curve will therefore slope fairly steeply downwards (as D_3 in Fig. 4.3). Thus the slope of the demand curve or average revenue curve of the firm will have a significant downward slope – although less than that of the industry.

In the former cases of many firms in the market, the extent to which the demand curve slopes downwards is dependent on the degree to which the firms in the market succeed in differentiating their product so that, when the firms are chosen for, say, selective tendering, the client sees this group as producing a product significantly different from those of the non-selected group. If he does, then the firms have succeeded in carving off a little part of the total market and in forming a limited monopoly or oligopoly in it. In this case this part of the market becomes in effect a new market on its own and the demand curves of the individual firms will be related to the demand curves in the market. However, as other contractors have products which are fairly close substitutes for theirs, the slope of the new minimarket demand curve will be rather elastic and therefore the slope of the derived demand curves of the individual firms within the market will slope only very slightly – perhaps insignificantly – downwards on account of the market situation. This means that in order to get to the stage of persuading more clients to buy his particular variety of contracting, the contractor will have not only to persuade them of its merits but also to make its price attractive as well. Similarly, if his price is rather high, he will lose a large number of potential clients. It is important to realise that this particular price persuasion operates mainly when the client is considering which contractor to short-list. In the actual price-determination situation the position is rather different.

TENDERING DATA AS AN INDICATION OF THE SLOPE OF THE
AVERAGE REVENUE CURVE

The practical extent of competition may be looked at in a different way. If a firm is at a given point on its average revenue
curve, i.e. had been, say, putting in tenders with a mark-up of
3 per cent and had obtained 100 units of business, the entrepreneur could probably give an answer to the question: If you had
put in a mark-up of 1 per cent, what volume of business would
you have obtained, and what would it have been with a 5 per
cent mark-up? At the lower price the firm would probably have
obtained more business and at the higher price less business.

Data on tender prices (Lea *et al.*, 1972)[5] show that a $2\frac{1}{2}$ per
cent change in the price at which a bid is placed would have a
substantial effect on the volume of business obtained. This
means that the slope of the average revenue or demand curve
is small. All that this tells the contractor, however, is that if
he *consistently* put in a price including a mark-up of 5 per cent
he would obtain, say, 1,000 units of business, whereas, if he
consistently over the same period put in bids with a $2\frac{1}{2}$ per cent
mark-up he would obtain, say, 2,000 units of business. It does
not tell him for any particular contract what price he should
quote in order to obtain the work.

Possible reasons for a wide range of tender prices for any contract are, firstly, that the estimators of the various firms do not
agree on the likely cost of the project. This is discussed in detail
in Chapter 13 but the range of cost estimates is frequently substantial. Secondly, the contractors may have different levels of
cost, i.e. some are substantially more efficient, and therefore
have lower costs, than others. This is possible but difficult to
assess in view of the fact that they cannot estimate their costs
accurately and the difference in costs is probably small compared with the differences due purely to wrong estimates.
Thirdly, the competitors may be at different points on their
cost curves. Fourthly, the contractors may have added widely
different mark-ups for overheads and profits. Assuming that
they would like to obtain the contract, this implies that they
have very diverse estimates of the market price. It should be
noted that the first and fourth of these reasons are incompatible
with assumptions of perfect knowledge in perfect competition,

and that all imply substantial differences in the cost curves of the firm and/or of entrepreneurial ability.

NON-RESALEABLE PRODUCT AND SINGLE-PROJECT MARKET

The contractor is in a different position from manufacturing industry in that he sells his product, i.e. the service of assembly, etc., to a particular client, but that once that service is sold, it ceases by its very nature to exist in that form and becomes embodied in the building (or other work) which is created. This building is custom-built, i.e. it is built at a specific place and in a particular way for the client for whom it is intended. The client can sell this building to someone else, but (leaving aside the effects of inflation) it would normally be expected to be less valuable to the other person, because it was not designed especially for him. The client cannot resell the services of the contractor because they have been used up. Thus as in the case of other services such as doctors' advice, there is no market in which resale can take place. This means that the contractor has some of the advantages of a discriminating monopolist. In a limited sense, each price-determining situation, i.e. the tender or the negotiation, for a single building is a temporary market and the contractor can get as high a price as possible in this market with no risk that the client with whom the bargain is struck can resell the same product, i.e. the service, in another market. But in this one-project market there is no average revenue curve and no marginal revenue curve, for there is no possibility of varying the units of output which will be sold. It is an all-or-nothing situation. Moreover, the price fixed in this one-project market does not affect the price of previously struck bargains in other markets. It is in the contractor's interest to make the price as high as possible while still obtaining the contract. This is dealt with in some detail in Chapter 13. In more general terms it is elaborated in Chapter 14, where revenue and costs are considered together to determine how a contractor may best attain his objectives.

13 Price Determination for a Single Project

In the construction industry price is determined for large indivisible lumps of work, each one of which represents a large proportion of the work load on the contractor (see Chapter 7) or of the part of the organisation operating in a particular market. The most usual method of this price determination is some form of tendering (see Table 7.1), but negotiation in various forms also plays its part. Neither fits easily into the usual mould of the economics of price determination, and in this chapter the process will be analysed. After an introductory section on risk and uncertainty, the pricing process is divided into three decision stages described against the background of tendering. The theoretical approach for all three of the stages is based on Shackle's (1952)[1] conception of degree of potential surprise. Then alternative theories, notably the probability approach, are investigated, and finally consideration is given to the analysis of price negotiation.

RISK AND UNCERTAINTY

It will be seen in the analysis which follows that risks and uncertainties facing the contractor, both in the estimates of the costs of the project and in the reactions of his competitors to the same tender situation, must play a large part in the assessment of the price to be quoted. This is not surprising when it is considered that the contractor is gauging the correct price for a project not yet built, for which he may not have seen detailed drawings, on a site of which he may have no knowledge, and with a labour work-force not yet organised. It is perhaps surprising that any firm price can be quoted at all.

Before embarking on a discussion of the tendering situation, the distinction between risk and uncertainty must be clarified.

Risk arises when the assessment of the probability of a certain event is statistically possible. Risk is insurable. Uncertainty arises when the probability of the occurrence or non-occurrence of an event is indeterminate. Uncertainty is not insurable (Knight, 1921).[2] There are sufficient records of rainfall for the month of November to make an assessment of the probability of its raining on ten days in that month, and insurance cover could be obtained. On the other hand, the soil conditions 100 feet down over a given area of one acre in the Amazon basin are not known and are the subject of uncertainty. It would not be a subject for insurance.

There is no hard-and-fast line between risk and uncertainty. The occurrence of some events may be moved from the category of uncertainty to that of risk by better information. Indeed, unknown data may be divided into three categories:

(*a*) data which cannot be known;

(*b*) data which are not known but could with research be obtained;

(*c*) data which, although known, are not available to the decision-maker, either because they are merely inaccessible or because he is incapable of understanding them.

Each category may be subject either to risk or to uncertainty. It cannot be known whether it will rain on more than ten days in November in the year 2000, and this would have been a matter of uncertainty before weather records were kept. It is now a matter of risk – at least to those who are aware of the possibility of probability calculation or insurance policies. Similarly, the soil conditions in the Amazon basin are matters of uncertainty but could be transferred to the category of risk if sufficient borings were undertaken to determine probabilities of the area in question having certain characteristics.

Data which could be obtained by research include, for example, the cost to the firm of estimating for a certain tender. This is a matter of uncertainty until the research has been carried out, and then of certainty.

The past tender prices of competitors may not be known by a contractor because he has not maintained records and are therefore the subject of uncertainty. Data on how to use them when he has them may not be available to him, and indeed he may be incapable of understanding them.

Many of the objectives of decision theory in its application to tendering are to remove events from the area of uncertainty to the area of risk or that of certainty.

THREE DECISION STAGES

The problems of the firm in the pricing situation may be divided into three, and these will be considered here as three stages in the decision-making process:

STAGE 1: COST OF UNDERTAKING THE PROJECT

Although the estimating process goes into detail on the cost of items in the bill of quantities, in fact contractors cannot judge accurately what the cost of a project will be. Some of the many possible reasons for variations in costs are listed below. It will be seen that most of these are uncertainties, i.e. they are not insurable but a part or the whole of some of these may be shifted on to the client or other participators in the construction process.

1. Labour costs:
   (*a*) Bad morale, go-slows or strikes, and hence poor productivity – uncertainty.
   (*b*) Inadequate pre-planning of operations – uncertainty, but with adequate data could become risk.
   (*c*) Faulty workmanship due to untried labour force – uncertainty but could become risk.
   (*d*) Inadequate estimate for local wage costs including travelling time, etc. – uncertainty.
   (*e*) Inflation in wage costs – uncertainty, but may be partially shifted to client in fluctuating-clause contract.

2. Material costs:
   (*a*) Change in material prices over time – uncertainty, but can be shifted to client with a fluctuating-clause contract or hedged by buying in advance of requirements and storing, in which case becomes certainty but at a cost, i.e. storage costs.

(*b*) Shortage of materials or late deliveries – uncertainty, but can also be overcome by advance buying (see above) or better planning.

3. Subcontracting costs:
   Subcontractor not performing as required – uncertainty, only redress is from subcontractor himself.

4. Bill of quantities items:
   (*a*) Arithmetical error – uncertainty, but this is usually checked by client's quantity surveyor and adjustment or withdrawal may be allowed.
   (*b*) Variations in the quantities in the bill. If the items are correctly priced this should not be too serious, but an item may be under- or overpriced in error or in an attempt by the contractor to anticipate an over- or underestimate in the quantities, and weight his bill accordingly. There is a danger that the estimator may have anticipated wrongly – uncertainty.
   (*c*) The bill item unit of measure being different from the supplier's unit of measure. Such is the case, for example, where the supplier provides backfill material by weight and the client pays by volume (McKirdy, 1971)[3] – uncertainty.
   (*d*) Likelihood of mistakes using complex bills. Fine and Hackemer (1970)[4] have shown that there is considerable variability in estimating, but they and Grinyer and Whittaker[5] have shown that this variability can be assessed and expressed mathematically – risk.

5. Soil conditions:
   Soil conditions being different from those expected. This may in certain circumstances be the responsibility of the client; if not, uncertainty.

6. Management costs:
   Inadequate quality of management. This is not important with tried management personnel, although a man may be a good manager on, say, a technically complex project and not on one where labour unrest develops. The greatest problem is in a rapidly expanding firm

where the management quality is to some extent unknown – uncertainty.

7. Weather and seasons:
   Bad weather can seriously hamper the progress of a job. It can be insured against or it can be to some extent overcome at a cost by winter building precautions – risk.

8. Actions of designers:
   (*a*) Architect or engineer not supplying detailed drawings on time – uncertainty, but can be shifted to client except to the extent that cost of disruption of the contract cannot be proved for a claim. On one large London site the disruption caused by lack of drawings was a main factor in starting a chain of events, including serious labour troubles which ultimately shut the site.
   (*b*) Architect or engineer changing mind – uncertainty, but with proviso in (*a*) above can be shifted to the client.

9. Catastrophes:
   Fire, flood, etc. – risks which can be insured.

10. Overrunning of time:
   The contract not completed on time and penalty clause involved – uncertainty.

Most of these factors are not considered in the estimator's assessment of cost, but are added later when the decision is finally taken on the tender price. They should, however, be considered by the entrepreneur as part of the assessment of cost, and, in addition, to arrive at the real cost of the job he should include an allowance for the opportunity cost of the capital locked up using discounted cash flow techniques.

In one way or another the contractor has to assess the extent of the remaining uncertainties in the total estimate of real cost (of which the estimator's part is given as a single figure even to the board of the contracting company) and to balance this uncertainty against the profit or loss that he might obtain. Contractors are not always successful in making this assessment. Hackemer (1970)[6] has stated that 'one division (of Richard Costain Ltd) with an average mark-up of just over 6 per cent manages to break even over the year.... Another division with an average mark-up of 8 per cent manages over the year a profit/turnover ratio of about 2 per cent.' How much of this divergence is accounted for by the variability due to the nature of the bill of quantities and how much to other uncertainties is not known.

Some definite relationships would be expected between the anticipated costs attributable to risk and to the amount of management required on the one hand and various job characteristics on the other hand. The project characteristics of size, duration, intensity, proportion subcontracted, proportion of labour costs relative to other costs and complexity will be considered.

Broemser (1968)[7] has investigated this field and has postulated that a large job in relation to a contractor's capacity implies an increase in risk and that therefore the contractor would add a higher mark-up to cover this. At the small end of work the requirement of the management would be great, but at the same time the management could be better employed on larger jobs – hence its opportunity cost on small jobs is high. Therefore the cost/size relationship would be expected to be U-shaped.

The effect of duration is expected to be similar, as increasing duration beyond a certain point also involves a high element of risk and hence a rise in percentage mark-up. At the same time a short-period job may not be worth the management effort.

Perhaps more important is intensity of work measured by the size/duration ratio (slightly different from the measure discussed by Broemser). A high size/duration ratio implies a very tight working schedule with increased costs of management, overtime, etc., while a low one implies that management is too thinly used. It seems that in this relationship too, costs will rise from their low position at optimum intensity to higher levels below and above the optimum level to form a U-shaped curve.

Broemser also suggests that the more work a contractor subcontracts to others, the lower will be his risk and hence the lower his percentage mark-up on the value of the whole contract, except that where he does only a small part of the work himself, this will require an inordinate amount of management time and hence there will be a lower limit to his overall mark-up.

Benjamin (1969)[8] discusses Broemser's work and also considers other relationships. He associates high risk with a high proportion of labour costs and with winter or wet-season working, and hence concludes that in these circumstances mark-ups will be higher. He also points out that high penalties for late completion will have a substantial effect on the mark-up required.

There is another factor which must be considered, namely that of the complexity of the project, and this is not explicitly examined either by Broemser or by Benjamin. It might be expected that the cost associated with risk would increase with complexity of the project and therefore that the difference between the cost of all inputs and the overall cost would rise as the complexity of the product increases.

Most of these factors are not such that the client would wish to take them into consideration in drawing up his brief. The exception is the duration of the job, and hence its intensity. Consider first the situation in which the client wishes to occupy the building at a particular date – say a school to be available in August for September. If he has the building earlier he will incur interest charges on the capital for the whole project when he expected to build up to this figure only in August. These additional costs are shown in Fig. 13.1 as linear, i.e. *CD*. In fact, taking into account the discounted value over time they would not be linear, but this problem has been ignored in this diagram for the sake of simplicity. If the client has the building later than August he will lose all the advantages of September occupation and the opportunity cost of not having the building will rise sharply as *DE*. On the other hand, in the situation in which the client wishes to use the building as soon as possible and will obtain rent for it (or save rent elsewhere), the rise in opportunity cost will be linear as *FG*.

The contractor's costs are, as already explained, as *AB* in Fig. 13.1, with optimum completion time *P*. The client will have to bear the contractor's costs as well in a higher mark-up, so he wishes to minimise the value of *AB* + *CE* or *HJ* in the first situation and the optimum completion time will then be at *K*. In the second situation he wishes to minimise the value of *AB* + *FG* or *LM* and the optimum completion time will be at *N*.

Under the present system, in general, neither the client nor the contractor knows the time/cost curves of both of them, and the chances of arriving at the optimum time are slight. It would be sensible for these time data as well as cost data to be taken into account in selecting the contractor.

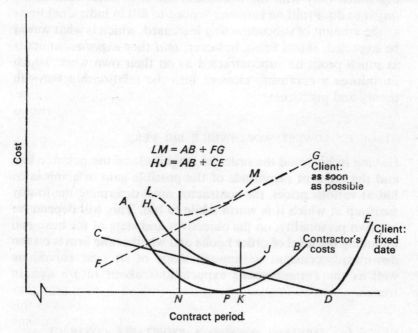

FIG. 13.1. Additional costs associated with time

It is not only what contractors *ought* to add as mark-up, but also what they actually do, which is of interest. In the case of percentage profit made in relation to size of contract, Fine (1970)[9] found that, in general, the larger the contract the smaller the percentage profit. Barnes (1972)[10] found little overall correlation between contract size and gross profit, although the five larger companies had higher profits in their smaller contracts. He found too that the majority of companies showed their highest profit in their dominant size range.

On intensity of work, the Building Economics Research Unit (1972)[11] has found in its preliminary analysis that the larger firms worked at a greater intensity than smaller ones for the same size project. This supports the view that it is the size or intensity in relation to the capacity of the firm which is important rather than any absolute measure.

The Ashridge study (1972)[12] came to some interesting conclusions about the relationship between profits and subcontracting which tally with the discussion above of what contractors *ought* to do. Profit on turnover tended to fall in individual firms as the amount of subcontracting increased, which is what would be expected. (Most firms, however, *said* they *expected* to make as much profit on subcontracted as on their own work, which introduces a confusing element into the relationship between theory and practice!)

STAGE II: LOWEST WORTHWHILE BID PRICE

Having in his mind the order of magnitude of the possible loss and the order of magnitude of the possible gain in going in to bid at various prices, the contractor must determine the lowest mark-up at which it is worth while to bid. This will depend on his own personality, on the objectives and state of the business, including the level of order books and whether the firm is on the downward, constant or upward slope of its cost curves, as well as the entrepreneur's expectations about future market trends.

STAGE III: TOWARDS WINNING A PROFITABLE CONTRACT

Having decided that he would like to obtain a contract at a certain minimum price, the entrepreneur must then balance the various prices and mark-ups he could put in against the likelihood of obtaining the job at these prices.

The likelihood of obtaining the job at any price will depend on (a) the number of competitors bidding and their identity, (b) the state of the order books of these competitors and the point they are at on their cost curves, and (c) their expectations.

Clearly, the contractor cannot have perfect knowledge of how all his competitors are faring. Much of the work on bidding theory attempts to bring this uncertain situation to a risk situation by basing the assessment of competitor's tender price on the past data of how competitors have tendered in the past. This will be explained and discussed in more detail in the review of bidding models.

Stage I on the cost of undertaking the project and stage III have a very high degree of uncertainty in them, and all stages, but particularly stage II, are very closely bound up with the overall state of the business and with the character and personality of the contractor/entrepreneur. In order to analyse these stages in more detail, use is made of ideas and concepts developed by Shackle in a number of publications (e.g. 1952[1] and 1955[13]), and his type of analysis is adapted to the specific construction industry tendering situation.

THEORETICAL ANALYSIS OF THE THREE STAGES

STAGE I: COST OF UNDERTAKING THE PROJECT

The Degree of Potential Surprise

Shackle's analysis is based on the degree of potential surprise, i.e. the surprise or shock which would be felt by a person at the occurrence of an event about which uncertainty had existed. This is applied to the assessment of the uncertainty of the cost estimates of a project. In Fig. 13.2, on the horizontal axis are

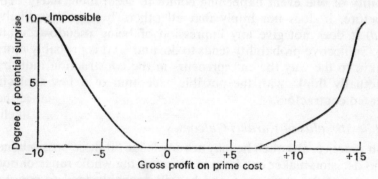

FIG. 13.2. Degree of potential surprise at a bid $x + 5$ making levels of profit or loss

measured the losses or profits which may be made with a given bid. On the vertical axis is measured the degree of potential surprise which would be registered by the entrepreneur at each of these possible losses and profits. The degree of potential surprise ranges from no surprise to the greatest surprise which can be experienced, i.e. from certainty to impossibility. An arbitrary scale of 0–10 has been adopted. Thus the entrepreneur regards it as impossible (degree of potential surprise of 10) that bid $x + 5$ (x being his estimated cost and 5 his percentage profit) will produce a loss as high as 10 per cent or a profit of 15 per cent, but perfectly possible, i.e. would not be surprised at all (hence degree of potential surprise of 0), if it produced anything from a loss of 2 per cent to a profit of 7 per cent. At ranges between 2 per cent and 10 per cent loss and between 7 per cent and 15 per cent profit, he would experience varying degrees of potential surprise.

The concept of degree of potential surprise is much less precise than that of probability analysis, but probability analysis is not applicable to this particular situation because, as already shown, most of the variable factors are uncertainties to which no probability can be assigned and of which the assessment is largely qualitative, not quantitative.

The advantages of the degree of potential surprise are that (a) it is applicable to situations not susceptible to probability analysis; (b) it recognises that for the entrepreneur a number of outcomes are all perfectly and equally possible; (c) if the possibility of one event happening comes to seem more likely than before, it does not imply that all others become less likely; (d) it does not give any impression of being pseudo-accurate as subjective probability tends to do; and (e) it is probably more akin to the way the entrepreneurs in the construction industry actually think, with the possible exception of a few sophisticated contractors.

The Stimulus of Various Outcomes

In practice, although he may acknowledge all these possibilities, no decision-maker can keep in his mind the whole range of outcomes at the same time, and he will probably tend to concentrate his attention on one possible level of profit and one possible level of loss with their relevant degrees of potential surprise. These will stimulate his imagination. He will fix on them just as a man filling in the football pools will choose, according to his temperament, to go for small gains with high chances of obtaining them or large gains with tiny possibilities of realisation or somewhere in between. These will be the examples of potential gain or loss which would be used in board discussions. In order to understand the theoretical basis of the selection of the points of stimulus, Shackle's concept of stimulus indifference curves can be used with special application to the bid situation.

A stimulus indifference curve is the locus of points where the stimulus to the imagination of the entrepreneur afforded by a combination of surprise and profit or loss is constant. In Fig. 13.3 these stimulus indifference curves are shown by the dotted

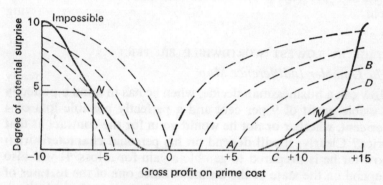

FIG. 13.3. Stimulus indifference curves and the degree of potential surprise at outcome bid $x + 5$

lines. The decision-maker will receive equal stimulus on, say, indifference curve AB from a profit of 5 per cent with no degree of potential surprise and a profit of 10 per cent with about 5 points of degree of potential surprise and at all points along the curve. He will be more stimulated – and therefore be on a higher indifference curve – by a higher profit of, say, 8 per cent with no degree of potential surprise (point C on indifference curve CD). Similarly, he will have stimulus indifference curves relating degree of potential surprise to loss.

This stimulus indifference map may be superimposed on the degree of potential surprise curves (Fig. 13.2), as it has been in Fig. 13.3. The point on which the entrepreneur will focus his attention will be that giving him the greatest stimulus, i.e. where his highest stimulus indifference curve is tangential to the degree of potential surprise curve, at N and M in Fig. 13.3. In this case the highest stimulus would be obtained by a profit of 12 per cent combined with a degree of potential surprise of $2\frac{1}{2}$ and a loss of 6 per cent with a degree of potential surprise of $4\frac{1}{2}$.

In order to standardise the degree of potential surprise in comparing profit and loss, the entrepreneur can move along the stimulus indifference curve to nil degree of potential surprise. The value of the profit with this nil degree of potential surprise is called the standardised focus gain, and the corresponding value of the loss with nil degree of potential surprise is called the standardised focus loss. The standardised focus gain would then be 9 per cent profit and the standardised focus loss 4 per cent.

STAGE II: LOWEST WORTHWHILE BID PRICE
The Gambler Indifference Map

How can a businessman decide, when he has in mind a perfectly possible profit of 9 per cent and a perfectly possible loss of 4 per cent, whether or not he would go in for the contract at that price? Clearly, it will depend on his personal characteristics – how far he is prepared to gamble a gain for a loss. It will also depend on the state of the business. Since one of the features of construction is that any one contract forms a relatively large part of the firm's annual turnover, the decision on any one contract is an important determinant of the profit or loss for the year. Hence the decision-maker cannot rely on gains and losses offsetting each other in the period relevant to him (if he could, he could simply say a standardised focus gain of x per cent is greater than the standardised focus loss and therefore it would be worthwhile at that price).

Moreover, his reaction to the chances of loss or gain will be to some extent determined by other objectives of the business. The entrepreneur may, for instance, wish to obtain a particular contract because it carries personal prestige. If he has a contract manager whom he especially wants to keep and for whom this job is eminently suitable, he may be more prepared to stand a loss.

It is unlikely in practice that the process of estimating costs takes into account the position of the firm on its cost curve, although it seems, from a survey carried out by Goodlad (1972),[14] that the industry is becoming convinced of the value of marginal costing techniques in tendering. In any case the entrepreneur does consider his cost function explicitly or implicitly after the initial assessment of costs in the decision on what mark-up to apply if the firm is on the downward slope of its cost curve. If the overheads are not spread over a sufficient volume of work, the entrepreneur will be more prepared to take the work than if the firm's capacity is becoming fully stretched.

Two individuals may react quite differently to the same situation. If, to take an extreme example, the company is on the verge of insolvency, one man may be prepared to risk all on one large contract which could pull the firm through completely but could be disastrous, while another man will hope for a number of less risky jobs and be prepared to wait years for financial viability rather than become insolvent.

In short, each decision-maker will have his own gambler indifference map, as suggested by Shackle, reflecting partly his own personality and partly the state of the business. It may change with every change in the state of the business and hence with every new contract won. Such a gambler indifference map is shown in Fig. 13.4. The indifference curves take the shape to be expected with two variables, one of which is desirable and the other undesirable.

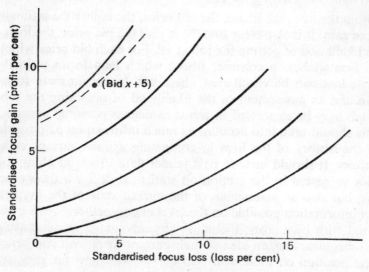

FIG. 13.4. Gambler indifference map

The values of the standardised focus gain and the standardised focus loss, derived from stage II in the decision process, may be plotted on the gambler indifference map. If the point falls on an indifference curve cutting the gain axis, the project is worthwhile to the firm at that price. If it falls on an indifference curve cutting the loss axis, it is not worthwhile. The standardised focus gain for bid $x + 5$ of 9 per cent and the standardised focus loss of 4 per cent would fall on an indifference curve cutting the gain axis at $6\frac{1}{2}$ per cent. This value might be called the ultimate focus gain, since it is that derived after taking into account both the stimulus indifference curve and the gambler indifference curve, i.e. stage I and stage II in the decision process.

All this analysis of bid price in relation to the firm has been undertaken in respect of one bid price, $x + 5$. Similar analysis can be undertaken for prices above and below $x + 5$, i.e. $x - n, \ldots, x-3, x-2, x-1, x+1, x+2, x+3, \ldots, x+n$. For each bid price there will be an ultimate focus gain or loss and each can be plotted on the one gambler indifference map.

STAGE III: TOWARDS WINNING A PROFITABLE CONTRACT

Likelihood of Getting the Job

Within the firm, the higher the bid price, the higher the ultimate focus gain. It is also clear that the higher the bid price, the lower the likelihood of getting the job at all. For each bid price which the firm wishes to consider (those which lead to an ultimate focus loss can be eliminated) there will be an ultimate focus gain and an assessment of the likelihood of obtaining the job, which may be expressed in terms of degree potential surprise. This should take into account as much information as possible on the history of the firm in competing against various competitors. It should include past tender data arranged along the lines suggested in the section on statistical decision theory below, but also an assessment of the overall state of the market, any information possible on the level of competitors' costs compared with own costs, including any advantage in purchasing or subcontracting, an idea of their current work load and hence their position on their own cost curves, and how far they are likely for other reasons to want the job.

Bidding Indifference Map

Just as the decision-maker had a gambler indifference map balancing loss against gain, so he will have an indifference map balancing degree of potential surprise of getting the contract against ultimate focus gain if he does. This might be named a bidding indifference map.* Its shape will be governed principally by the state of the firm's order books, an assessment of how the market price is likely to change in the future and of contracts coming on to the market in the future. Fig. 13.5 illustrates the bidding indifference map of a contractor motivated to maximise profits.

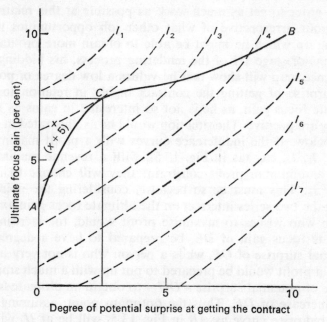

FIG. 13.5. Bidding indifference map

For each bid price the ultimate focus gain and degree of potential surprise can be plotted as AB in Fig. 13.5. Bid $x + 5$, for example, is plotted at ultimate focus gain of $6\frac{1}{2}$ per cent and degree of potential surprise of $\frac{1}{2}$ (on a scale 0–10). The

*The analysis here is a further development from that of Shackle.

curve of bid prices on this map may be very varied in shape, since it is determined by so many factors, but it may retain some of the shape of the normal degree of potential surprise curve. Line AB is tangential to the highest indifference curve at C, giving an ultimate focus gain of $7\frac{1}{2}$ per cent and a degree of potential surprise of obtaining the contract of $2\frac{1}{2}$. This will correspond to a bid price substantially higher than $x + 5$.

Alternative Objective of the Firm

If the entrepreneur wished to obtain only normal profit and thereafter to maximise turnover, his strategy would be somewhat different. He would need to obtain on each contract a minimum level of profit, and the contractor would tender or negotiate in order to get as much work as possible at this relatively low profit, irrespective of what other job opportunities were coming up which he might be able to obtain more profitably. In terms of stage III of the tendering process, his bidding indifference map will show that he values a low degree of potential surprise of getting the contract highly in relation to the ultimate focus gain, as he is not so interested in gains as long as they are positive. The situation would be as illustrated in Fig. 13.6 below. If the indifference curves with a profit maximiser are I_1, I_2, I_3, etc. (as in Fig. 13.5), with a revenue maximiser (with a minimum profit constraint they will change to, say, J_1, J_2, J_3. This must be so because, considering the point D where the two series intersect on the ultimate focus gain axis, a person who wishes to maximise profit would, for increase in ultimate focus gain of DE, be prepared to have a degree of potential surprise of OF, while a person who is not very interested in profit would be prepared to put up with a much smaller degree of potential surprise – OG – to obtain an ultimate focus gain increase of DE. Thus the optimum point, assuming the same bid-price curve as AB in Fig. 13.5, will be at H, with a lower ultimate focus gain combined with a lower degree of potential surprise for the revenue maximiser than for the profit maximiser.

VALUE OF THE ANALYSIS

Thus this analysis tries, firstly, to develop a theory of the stages of thought-processes through which entrepreneurs go, consciously or unconsciously, in coming to a decision on tendering, and secondly, by bringing these stages and a possible method of analysis to the forefront of the entrepreneur's mind, it tries to provide a framework to help the more sophisticated entrepreneur to analyse and improve his decisions. It is not suggested that entrepreneurs should now spend their time drawing their degree of potential surprise curves and their stimulus, gambler

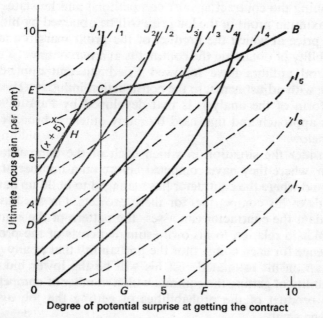

FIG. 13.6. Bidding indifference map: alternative assumptions

and bidding indifference maps, although it would probably be possible for entrepreneurs to indicate where they were on such maps. It is, however, suggested that the analysis would be helpful in understanding the reason for decisions on tender prices; in locating the reasons for differences of opinion between persons sharing the entrepreneurial function within contracting firms; in assessing how far the bidding theory based on the probability approach can help in tendering decisions; and hence, altogether, in making the process of tender decisions more logical and efficient.

STATISTICAL DECISION THEORY

PROBABILITY APPROACH

Most of the theoretical work on the bidding situation has been developed in the United States on the basis of the probability approach, starting with Friedman's article in 1956.[15] His model concentrates on stage III of the analysis, i.e. on the probability of winning the contract against competitors, and he states that the maximum profit in the long run will be obtained by bidding at the price at which the product of the profit margin and the probability of obtaining the contract is at a maximum.

Several authors have followed Friedman and applied his model, with adjustments, to the construction industry. The simplest form of the analysis is that developed by Park (1966).[16] Park's approach and that used by many others is broadly outlined below.

Consider the situation in which each of the competitors is known, where they have competed before on a number of projects, and where the contractor has managed to build up data on the bids of his competitors for these projects. On the basis of these data the contractor can assess the pattern of the competitors' bids in relation to his own estimated costs of the projects and hence for each competitor the probability that at any given mark-up on his estimated cost his will be the lower bid. The probability of getting the contract with a number of competitors is the product of the probabilities of getting the job against each one singly.

In practice the competitors in a given situation are not always known. However, by adding the bids of any number of competitors, it is possible to arrive at a probability of winning against an average or typical competitor.

The argument is that, assuming that the bids are independent, the maximum profit in the long run will be obtained by bidding at the price at which the product of the profit margin and the probability of obtaining the contract is at a maximum. Although in a later article Park (1968)[17] adds the variable of job size to this analysis, he concentrates entirely on stage III of the process.

Benjamin (1972)[18] compares five of the bidding models available in the United States in the way in which they estimate costs and expected profit and in the way they assess probability of winning. In this paper, therefore, he concentrates on stage III of the process.

DISCUSSION OF THE PROBABILITY APPROACH FOR STAGE III ANALYSIS

It seems clear and acceptable that the determination of the probability of getting a job using past data is a very valuable piece of information for a firm to have, and as the tender prices are usually public – although the name of the contractor for each bid may not be – there is little practical difficulty in obtaining the data to arrive at a typical competitor probability distribution. Indeed, these data should be regarded as vital information to determine the degree of potential surprise to be assigned to getting the job at various prices. Moreover, the contribution of this approach is useful in its own right because it has been shown to yield better results in tendering than those which would have obtained by purely 'hunch' methods. If, however, it is intended to be used together with the expected profit concept as the major means of assessing the right price to quote, it is essential to be clear as to exactly what assumptions are being made.

The method assumes that the firm has knowledge of a sufficient number of tenders within the same market to make it possible to obtain reliable probability assessments. The reliability of these assessments for use in tendering will depend on similar market conditions (i.e. similar ruling prices) obtaining over the period from the earliest tender price used to the present time. The maximum period it is reasonable to take will vary according to conditions at the time, but it may often be shorter than three months. Only a medium to large firm would have sufficient tenders in that period to make it a practical possibility, and then in only fairly large markets. Thus if a firm has ten new contracts in a given market per annum and on average obtains one in five tenders, it will have tendered for fifty jobs and have, say, 200 competitors' prices. In three months it will have fifty prices.

A firm relying wholly on this method of tendering is a market follower, not a market leader. If the market changes it may take the entrepreneur, say, 15–20 tenders to realise, and these represent a large proportion of normal annual tenders, and the firm's work load will suffer accordingly. Grinyer and Whittaker[5] have devised a way of overcoming this problem by asking the entrepreneur to estimate a market coefficient, i.e. the arithmetic mean of what competitors' bids will be. This has been tested in live situations and found to produce reasonable results; it is in fact reinstating individual judgement as an important factor in the situation.

For markets where there are fewer than fifty bids on which to base a probability calculation, the detailed approach has little merit. The contractor knows that the higher the price he quotes, the lower the chance he has of obtaining the work, and with a small number of past bids his hunch may be better than any statistical data. This will apply to markets in which the individual firm has a small percentage, e.g. the small firm or firm having just entered a new market, and to cases where the market itself is small or new, e.g. motorways just after the Second World War. A number of one-off projects such as hydro-electric work in Scotland will fall into the same category.

The concept of expected value (or profit) of the contract must also be used with caution. It seems to apply best to a situation in which the firm is bidding for every possible contract within the market in which it is operating and in which the number of contracts it obtains is immaterial so long as the overall, i.e. total, profit is high. This means that the entrepreneur has to obtain his best profit by – so to speak – spreading the profit he gets on the successful bids over all the bids he might have got but did not. In fact his actual profit is not the expected value at all, but the percentage mark-up on the contracts he actually gets. Unless he is already bidding for all possible contracts in the market in which he operates, he would be better off bidding for more contracts at a higher mark-up rather than lowering his price and bidding for the same number. This is also the conclusion of the more sophisticated bidding models.

Moreover, as has been argued earlier, whether a firm wishes to bid for a contract at a high potential profit and a low probability of success or a low potential profit and a high probability of success depends on a number of other factors, such as the stability of the firm and the temperament of the entrepreneur. This probability approach to the determination of the optimum bid is by itself insufficient.

A THREE-STAGE PROBABILITY AND UTILITY APPROACH

The nearest approach of any model to dealing with the three stages is that of Benjamin (1969).[8] He notes three elements in the competitive bidding problem: (*a*) a probability distribution to express the uncertainty of the cost of performing the work; (*b*) a non-linear utility function which scales the bidder's preferences for different amounts of money when the possibility of a loss is considered explicitly in the problem; and (*c*) a means of assessing the probability of winning the contract with different bid amounts. These three elements more or less correspond to the three stages outlined with the degree of potential surprise method above.

His list of factors which contribute to the uncertainty of the construction cost estimate overlaps with those listed under stage I above. He mentions subcontractors bids, material availability and costs, labour availability and productivity, methods of performing the work, season in which work is done, location of job, type of building or type of construction and supervisory talent. Benjamin examines ways in which the probabilities of these factors may be assessed. Basically, however, these factors are uncertainties, not risks, and it is questionable whether probability is the right tool.

Benjamin's utility function 'transforms the monetary value of the outcome to a different scale which satisfies the bidder's ordering of preferences for the different amounts of profit or loss that are possible with a given bid amount and a given probability distribution on the cost of performing the work'. This approach is now substantially developed by Willenbrock (1972)[19] using sophisticated analysis. Although the methodology is quite different, the problems correspond to those in Shackle's gambler indifference map.

For stage III, Benjamin considers two groups of variables that influence the bids of the bidder and his competitors. The first group includes characteristics of the job which determine the amount of profit the contractor would expect from the job because of the different levels of risk involved or because of the different levels of effort involved. These include the amount of the penalty relative to the cost estimate of the general contractor's own part of the job, estimated proportion of labour costs, season and duration of job as well as the percentage of the job subcontracted.

It seems that some of these items, although usually considered at the end of the contractor's decision process, ought really to be considered when the entrepreneur has received his estimator's cost assessment and when he is adding to or subtracting from this to take account of his own knowledge of the other real costs which have to be assessed, i.e. in stage I, and it is under this heading at the beginning of this chapter that these characteristics have been discussed.

The second group of variables are those of the 'bidding environment'. Matters such as the location of the job will already have been taken into account in terms of costs under labour management, etc., or should have been if the real costs have been determined. The same applies to type of owner and his designer. These factors are, however, relevant in determining how the competitors will view the situation and should therefore colour the entrepreneur's view of how far his competitors are likely to have different real costs from himself.

Benjamin acknowledges that the data are not available to feed practically relevant information into his model. It is doubtful whether it will ever be meaningful to try to feed such data into an equation. Most of the factors are so varied and qualitative that it seems better to use judgement for quite wide groups of variables together via, for example, the degree of potential surprise of an event occurring.

NEGOTIATION AND OTHER METHODS OF PRICE DETERMINATION

The analysis of price determination in this chapter has so far been presented entirely in terms of the tendering situation. Most of it, however, is equally relevant to other methods of pricing the product of the industry. Stage I and stage II of the process – the determination of cost and of the lowest worthwhile price at which the contractor would wish to undertake the job – apply equally to tendering and to negotiation, and the principle stands even for package dealing, although in this case design also has to be taken into account.

Stage III of the process is different. Before negotiation the contractor will have decided the lowest price he will accept, and during negotiation he will attempt to obtain the highest possible price while still getting the contract. The client will have in mind the highest price he is prepared to pay for the job and will have the objective of obtaining it for the lowest possible price while still maintaining the quality of the finished product. As indicated earlier in Chapter 12, in negotiation the contractor may be in a limited monopoly situation, although the client can negotiate with more than one contractor. The monopoly is limited by the knowledge that if the client does not like the way the negotiations are proceeding, either with regard to price or for any other reason, he can go to other firms in the market. Within this framework negotiation will take place and the final outcome will depend on how much each negotiator wishes to deal with the other, on the top and bottom limit to the range within which a deal can take place, and on the skill of the negotiators.

Marsh (1973)[20] has analysed the process in considerable detail. He stresses that the final outcome often depends as much on the individual motivation of the negotiators for the two sides as it does on objective or economic considerations. He deals with the question of time costs at some considerable length because they have an important bearing on the outcome of the negotiations. This supports the conclusion reached in Chapter 12 of the importance of the time and money already invested in negotiations on the level of supernormal profit which the contractor may be able to obtain.

14 Conclusions on Costs, Revenue and the Equilibrium of the Contracting Firm

Having completed a study of the costs of the firm and the industry (Chapters 9, 10 and 13) and of the demand facing the firm (Chapters 11–13) and the industry (Chapters 4–7), it is appropriate first to summarise the main findings and then to combine them and to draw some conclusions on the equilibrium position of the firm on the two main assumptions of the objectives of the firm, namely profit maximisation and maximisation of turnover with a profit constraint (Chapter 8).

SUMMARY OF FINDINGS ON COSTS

In the short run the average variable cost curve of the contracting firm will be U-shaped, because at very low outputs there are some difficulties in the efficient use of inputs, and at high outputs in the short run, in which the resources of head office and some site management are fixed, the managerial inefficiencies and organisational problems are likely to cause rising costs of the other inputs, particularly of manpower whose efficiency is especially dependent on good management.

Fixed costs are relatively small in traditional construction, but nevertheless they suffice to make very small outputs expensive, and hence the total average cost curves rise more steeply to the left of their lowest point and slightly less steeply to the right of it than was the case when only variable costs were considered.

There was some discussion of the postponable costs, namely

part of the normal return on the entrepreneur's labours, and some of the return on capital invested, depending on whether interest *must* be paid regularly, whether capital *can* be withdrawn from the business and whether the firm wishes to expand.

In the long run fixed costs can be altered and postponable costs must be met, but there is no reason why the long run should be a particular definite period of time or indeed the same for all factors. In the very long run technologies can be altered and new technologies developed, and in any case when there is a change in the level of fixed costs there will usually be a change in the technology used. The shape of the long-run cost curve is uncertain. There are theoretical reasons, particularly the shortage of entrepreneurial ability and the possible inelasticity of factors of production, why the curve should eventually turn upwards, but instances of large and growing firms show that at least for some it is fairly flat over long ranges of output. Over time it may actually be sloping downwards because of improved technologies. In any case, because of the indivisibility of certain factors of production there are almost certainly humps in the long-run cost curve.

It seems fairly certain that there is a limit to the *rate* of growth of the firm, which means that as output increases or decreases over time the short-run curve is likely to be U-shaped. Moreover, the short-run cost curves are not reversible, in that the cost of increasing the level of output may be different from the costs of decreasing it.

In a consideration of the costs of the single project, the total number of which, over the whole period of their duration, determines the place of the firm on its average cost curve, it was found how extremely uncertain the real costs of a project are. Because of this, and because the contractor does not know in advance whether a certain contract will be obtained, there is uncertainty as to the actual level of his cost curves and of the point on them where he will be at a given time in the future.

SUMMARY OF FINDINGS ON REVENUE

The demand curves facing the contracting firm are determined by the demand curves facing the industry as a whole in all the various markets and the extent of competition in these markets.

It was found in the chapters on demands on the industry that the demand curves for all types of work were relatively inelastic. Thus if there were very few firms supplying these markets, the slope of their average revenue curves would be great and their monopoly power would be considerable.

In practice this is not the case, even in markets where there are relatively few contractors. At stages of the process of selection of contractors and of price determination where one or a few contractors are involved, the extent of the power of the contractor to act as a monopolist is limited by the ease with which other firms can enter that market and with which the client can increase the number of contractors involved. Overall there is little evidence of monopoly power in the industry, and such situations in which it exists account for a tiny proportion of the work of the industry as a whole. Thus the demand curve actually facing the contractor is likely on these arguments to be fairly elastic.

This is supported by a consideration of the tendering situation where, if a contractor consistently puts in tender prices with a low mark-up, he will get more business than if he puts in a high mark-up. Thus his demand curve cannot be horizontal as under perfect competition. However, if the contractor is not tendering for all the work in the market in which he operates, he would be better off (in spite of the small increase in his cost curves due to higher estimating costs) by tendering for more contracts at the same price than by lowering his price on the same number of tenders. If, therefore, he is able in some circumstances to obtain more work at the same price, his demand curve must be near to the horizontal perfect competition model.

If, however, the contractor is already tendering for all possible work without a given market, then, subject to the safeguard of ease of entry to any market, the average revenue curve may slope rather more steeply. Another possibility is that the contractor in such a market may have a kinked demand curve, i.e. that if he lowers his price the other contractors will take this into consideration in their assessment of the chances of obtaining work in the tendering situation and lower their price still further. If he raises his price, however, there will be no particular reaction on the part of his competitors.

SYNTHESIS OF COSTS AND REVENUE: SHORT RUN

Combining the likely cost curves of the firm with its probable revenue curve it is possible, following the analysis of Chapter 11, to see the way in which the firm maximises its profits. In Fig. 14.1A are shown the average revenue curve, *AR*, the marginal revenue curve *MR*, the average cost curve *AC* and marginal cost curve *MC* of the firm. Assume that the cost curve relates to the period of time in which it includes normal return on the entrepreneur's labours plus normal return on capital which can be withdrawn from the business but in which the fixed factors of management and head office cannot be altered. Then the output which maximises profit in this period is that at which marginal revenue equals marginal cost, i.e. at *A* in Fig. 14.1A, at which price is 210 and output about 4·6 units.

The output which maximises revenue making this level of normal profit is that at which average cost, including normal profit, equals average revenue, or point *B* in Fig. 14.1A, at price 125 and output about 8 units.

In Fig. 14.1B is shown the same situation in terms of total costs and total revenue. This presentation is more helpful when some additional level of profit is looked for other than the normal profit included in the cost curves. The difference between the total revenue curve and the total cost curve is profit (in excess of normal profit) and is plotted as *TP*. Thus the output which maximises profit is about 4·6 units, as was found from Fig. 14.1A, and that where there is no profit above normal profit is 8 units. If the entrepreneur wishes to obtain some level of profit below the maximum, in order, for example, to give more benefits to his employees, the output which he needs to obtain this level of profit is clearly ascertainable. Thus if he wishes to obtain a profit of, say, 200 above that included in the cost, combined with as high a level of turnover as possible, then he should be at *C* where his output will be about 7·3 units.

It was seen in Chapter 13 that the mark-up appropriate to any particular tender depends on a number of factors, including the state of the firm's order books, and where they expect to be on their cost curves relating to the period over which the work on the contract will extend. A study of the relationship of the marginal cost and marginal revenue curves in Fig. 14.1A

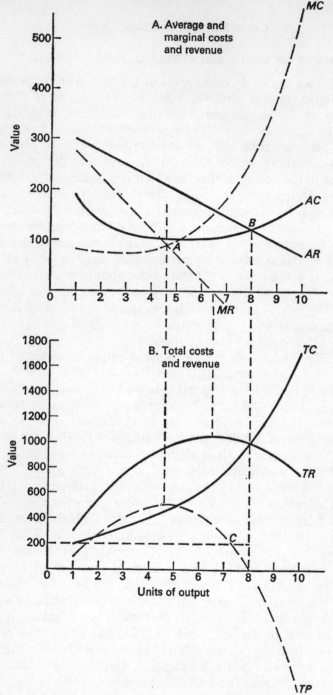

Fig. 14.1. Short-run equilibrium of the firm

shows how important this assessment can be. The difference between the marginal cost and marginal revenue at a point in time (say for practical purposes a month) varies greatly according to the work load, and therefore the mark-up which the contractor should contemplate to obtain that work also varies considerably. The situation is complicated by the fact that because of the irregular work load over time (see Fig. 9.2), the place on the cost curve will vary from month to month and yet a decision has to be taken for the contract as a whole. It is, however, clear that to adopt a policy of a constant mark-up is justified in only very special circumstances.

SYNTHESIS OF COST AND REVENUE: LONG RUN

In the long run the average cost curve of the contracting firm may, as suggested earlier, have a very stable overall level but with 'humps'. If this is so its situation would be rather as that shown in Fig. 14.2A, with AR_1 and MR_1 representing the average revenue and marginal revenue curves as before in Fig. 14.1A, and AC representing the humped average cost curve and MC the corresponding marginal curve. In this diagram the marginal revenue curve MR_1 cuts the marginal cost curve at A, at which the appropriate output is 4·8 units at which profits are maximised. In terms of total cost the situation is shown in Fig. 14.2B. TR_1 is the total revenue curve corresponding to the average and marginal revenue curves in Fig. 14.2A. TP is the total profit curve derived from $TR_1 - TC$, the total cost curve. Thus if the entrepreneur wanted to maximise profits he should not employ the new fixed factors necessary to expand output. If he wished to maximise revenue subject to making a normal profit he should move to point B with output 8·5 units, i.e. he should go over the 'hump'. If, however, he wished to make a minimum profit of 200 and have an output as large as possible subject to this constraint, he should expand his business over the hump but produce only 6 units of output.

The illustrations above are all in terms of the total revenue curve TR_1, which is derived from the average revenue curve in Fig. 14.2. If, however, the market is small and the entrepreneur has a large share of it, it is possible that he anticipates an upward shift in the demand curve so that it might become profit-

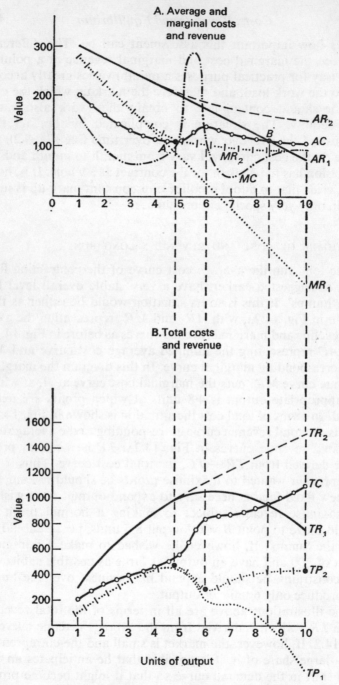

FIG. 14.2. Long-run equilibrium of the firm

able for him to expand output to be in a position to take advantage of this. Thus a contractor in a developing country producing housing might expect an expansion of demand so that the total revenue curve would shift upwards and to the right, thus making it more profitable to produce at larger outputs beyond the 'hump'.

In markets where the firm has a relatively small share, the total revenue curve may not turn down but over the relevant range of output continue to slope upwards at a rate faster than the total cost curve, as TR_2 in Fig. 14.2B with a total profit TP_2. There would be no optimum position within this range of output. This may be the state of some of the large contractors who have overcome most of the 'humps' and who could in any market which was large in relation to their output go on expanding both output and profit. As was seen under the heading 'Summary of Findings on Costs' above, there are reasons why in any market this state of affairs is unlikely to continue indefinitely.

Most contracting firms operate in several markets. The overheads of the business as a whole which cannot be allocated in any sensible way should be arbitrarily apportioned to the business in each market as fixed costs. In this way they will not affect the marginal cost. In order to maximise profit the firm should, in each market, operate at the output which equates marginal revenue and marginal cost. If the demand curves facing the individual firm are different in different markets or if their cost curves are different, this may result in charging a higher price in some markets than in others. As was seen in Chapter 12, this is possible because there cannot be a resale of the 'service' of construction.

APPENDIX

Indifference Curve Analysis Applied to the Demand for Housing

In Chapter 4 the demand for housing is considered, commencing with the concept of the individual's demand curve for units of housing. In this appendix the individual's demand curve is derived from his indifference curves.

The demand for housing depends initially on the consumer's assessment of the desirability of housing compared with all the other goods and services he could buy. Before embarking on indifference curves for housing, let us consider the general case of two commodities.

In Fig. A.1, curve I_1 is an indifference curve showing all the various combinations of commodity A and commodity B between which the consumer is indifferent or, to put it another way, which give him equal satisfaction. The consumer does not mind, for example, whether he has 15 units of commodity B and 3 units of commodity A, as at point C, or 4 units of commodity B and 10 of commodity A as at point D. If both commodities are desirable goods, indifference curves are convex to the origin as shown in Fig. A.1. Generally speaking, the more a person has of a commodity, the less value is placed on additional units of it. Thus to give up one unit of commodity B when he has only 4 units, the consumer needs 4 units of commodity A to compensate him. But when he has 15 units of commodity B, he needs only half a unit of commodity A to compensate him for the loss of one unit, i.e. to remain on the same indifference curve.

There will be an indifference curve for each level of consumer satisfaction. The higher the indifference curve, i.e. the further away from the origin, the greater the level of satisfaction. In

Fig. A.1, in moving from indifference curve I_1 to indifference curves I_2 and I_3, the consumer is able to have the same amount of one commodity and at the same time increase the amount of the other. Thus at E he has 20 units of commodity B and $2\frac{1}{2}$ of commodity A; at F on indifference curve I_2 he still has 20 units of B but in addition has 6 of A, i.e. $4\frac{1}{2}$ more than on indifference

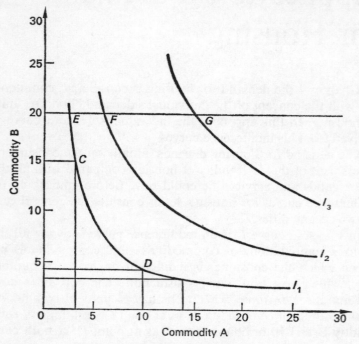

FIG. A.1. A consumer indifference map

curve I_1; and at point G he has the same amount of B with 15 of A. He is clearly better off at G than at F and at F than at E. In fact each consumer has an infinite number of indifference curves forming an indifference map, each curve being a contour on the hill of satisfaction. We cannot assign values to the contours because it is not possible to say that the consumer is, say, twice better off on a certain indifference curve than on another. All we know is that he becomes progressively better off as he goes 'up the hill'.

Going from the general case to the particular, we can put

housing on one axis and all other commodities on the other axis and consider the consumer's indifference map for housing and all other commodities. For present purposes, the simple assumption (discussed in Chapter 4) is made that one can some-how on a points system conceive of homogeneous units of housing, and these housing units are measured on the horizontal axis in Fig. A.2 as notional housing units consumed per annum. It is in practice difficult to measure 'all other goods'

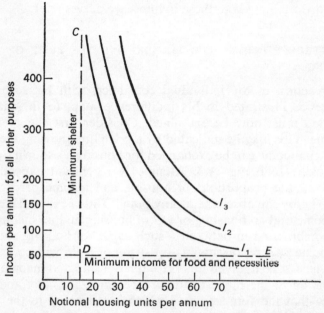

FIG. A.2. Indifference curves for housing and other commodities

except in terms of money, and therefore on the vertical axis all other goods are in money terms as annual income.

What can be said about the housing indifference map? First, the general shape of the curve will follow the usual indifference curve with two desirable goods. Housing, however, is special in that some minimum units of housing are very desirable and it is therefore likely that the curve with a low level of satisfaction will become asymptotic to a line parallel to the vertical axis. In other words, no matter how much income is given in compensation, there is a minimum standard of housing required. In

Fig. A.2 the indifference curves are shown as being asymptotic to a line parallel to the vertical axis, showing that the minimum number of units of housing at the level of satisfaction shown by indifference curve I_1 which are acceptable is 15. Similarly, the minimum income desired for other essential purposes such as food is shown as equivalent to 50 units of income per annum. The area between the axes and the lines *CD* and *DE* may in some sense be regarded as the area in which the standard of living is below acceptable social standards, at least as seen by the individual to whom these indifference curves refer.

INDIFFERENCE CURVES FOR HOUSING AND THE PRICE OF HOUSING

The reaction of the individual consumer, with his scales of preference illustrated in his indifference map, to the market situation must now be examined. Consider first the price of housing. This may be indicated by a price line showing the rate at which income can be exchanged for housing, as shown by, for example, *AB* in Fig. A.3. Along *AB* a constant expenditure will 'buy' the proportions of housing and income per annum as shown by the abscissae of any point. Thus he may have *OA* of income and no housing, or *OB* of housing and no income, or any combination in between – such as *DC* of housing and *CE* of income. *AB* represents his opportunities. He will be as well off as he can be if, given this price relationship and income *OA*, he gets on to the highest indifference curve possible, and this will be that indifference curve which is tangential to the price line *AB*. His optimum position will be at *C* where he will choose to have *OD* of income and *OE* of housing. The consumer has insufficient income to be at any other point than *C* on this indifference curve. If he were on another indifference curve, say at *F*, which is within his income, he would be better off by moving along the price line *AB* to *C*, because he is then on a higher indifference curve and therefore better off.

If the price of housing changes, the level of income remaining the same, the consumer will adjust so that at the new level of prices he is at his optimum position. If the price rises to *AG* the consumer will move from *C* to *H*. If it rises again to *AK* he will move to *J*.

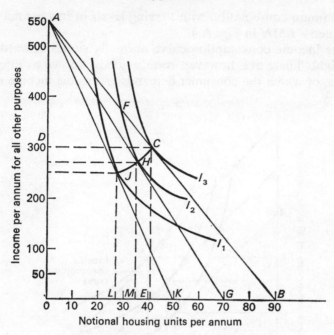

FIG. A.3. Indifference curves and price lines

The optimum points with each fresh price may be joined to form a price consumption curve *JHC* (sometimes known as an offer curve), showing how much will be consumed at each price.

CHANGES OF INCOME

At least as interesting as the change in the amount consumed at each price is the effect of a change in the consumer's income. This is particularly so as housing expenditure usually takes a large proportion of total income. In Fig. A.4 the increase is shown as a movement from *AB* to *CD* to *EF* in which the price relationship, shown by the slope of the lines, is constant and hence the income lines are parallel.

As income increases from *OA* to *OE*, the consumer changes from demanding *OG* housing and keeping *OJ* income to *OH* housing and keeping *OK* income. An income consumption curve (sometimes known as an Engel curve) joining the points

of optimum combination with varying levels of income may be
obtained – *LMN* in Fig. A.4.

The income consumption curve normally slopes upwards to
the right. There are, however, certain goods, known as inferior
goods, of which the consumer demands less as his income rises

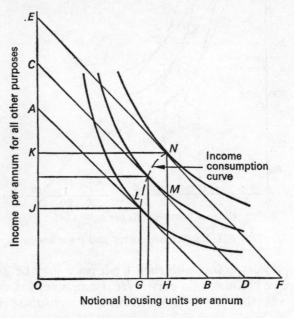

FIG. A.4. Indifference curves and income lines

because he replaces them by more luxurious commodities, and
in this case the income consumption curve slopes upwards to
the left. This situation could theoretically apply to housing if,
for example, very rich people chose to live in hotels or yachts
rather than in a normal dwelling. It is certainly unlikely to
apply for large groups of individuals.

EFFECT OF PRICE CHANGE: PART INCOME AND PART SUBSTITUTION EFFECT

The effect of a price change may be further analysed into (*a*)
the result of the price change of the commodity on the real

income of the consumer, and (b) the result of the price change in altering the relative prices of commodities.

If the price of housing falls, the consumer has in fact had an increase in his real income. This is illustrated in Fig. A.5. *AC* is the original price line with income of *OA*. This is tangential

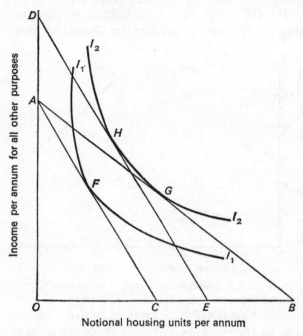

FIG. A.5. Income effect and substitution effect

to the indifference curve I_1 at F and F is the optimum point. Price then falls to AB. The new optimum position is G on indifference curve I_2. If the price had not changed, the consumer could have arrived at the indifference curve I_2 at H by an increase in income of AD, for DE is the price line parallel to AC representing this increase in income. The fall in price has given the consumer an increase in his real income of AD. In fact, because price has changed the consumer wishes to substitute the cheaper commodity for others and hence moves from H (the equilibrium point if income had increased with no price change) along his indifference curve I_2 to G.

THE DEMAND CURVE OF THE INDIVIDUAL CONSUMER

It is possible from the price consumption curve illustrated in Fig. A.3 to derive the consumer's demand curve showing how much of a commodity he will demand at various prices. Thus, deriving Fig. A.6 from Fig. A.3 at a price given by the slope of *AK*, i.e. *AO/OK*=550/50 i.e. 550 units of income for 50 units of housing or 11 units of income for 1 unit of housing, the

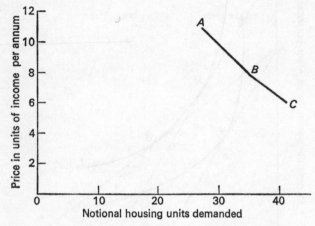

FIG. A.6. The demand curve of the individual

amount demanded is *OL*=27 units of housing; similarly, at a price given by the slope *AG*, i.e. 550/70 or 7·9 units of income for 1 of housing, the amount demanded is *OM*=35 units; at a price given by slope *AB*, i.e. 550/90 or 6·1 units for 1 unit of housing, the amount demanded is *OE*=41 units.

There is a further point to note, namely the relation of the price consumption curve to the demand curve of varying elasticities.

The price consumption curve shows the amount of income which will be devoted to a given commodity at various prices. In Fig. A.3 the price consumption curve rises as the price falls. This means that the consumer gives up less and less of his income with each fall in price – in other words, demand is inelastic. If the price consumption curve is falling, then demand is elastic, and if it is horizontal, the demand has an elasticity of 1.

THE EFFECT OF CAPITAL ON THE DEMAND FOR HOUSING

In the theoretical indifference curve analysis, homogeneous housing units have been considered as an alternative to all other goods (expressed as income per annum for all other purposes) and the price relationship is then expressed in terms of the price of housing per annum. The effect on demand of changes in income has been considered. In practice, housing may be rented or it may be bought, either with owned or borrowed capital. Most other goods – as represented on the vertical axis – are bought out of income rather than out of capital. Housing is a durable good with a high resale value and is therefore considered as a capital good.

There seem to be three main ways of dealing with the effect of capital ownership on the demand for housing:

(a) To do nothing: as income may be earned or derived from investments, i.e. capital, to consider income as an alternative to capital is already including some allowance for the capital component.

(b) To convert capital at the 'annuity rate': in order to increase the allowance for capital to its proper value in the decision to purchase a house over, say, twenty years, the capital could be converted to income at the 'annuity rate', i.e. capital depreciating to nil at the end of the period. This would conform to building societies' attitudes, although the allowed period of repayment is now greater than it was. This method requires knowledge of capital in private hands for which there is only one source, namely the Inland Revenue Statistics[1] based on estate-duty data. These include the total wealth of an individual at death but are not very reliable for capital lower than that subject to estate duty and are not representative of the population as a whole because they are based on property at death. Information on the value of investments is available for 1967 from a survey for the Building Societies Association (1968).[2] This, however, does not include all wealth and in particular does not include house ownership.

(c) To change the indifference map: the effect of capital is probably in any case not measured only by a discounting technique because a person with capital has more security and will therefore have a different attitude to committing a large amount of money. The best solution may therefore be to consider income as in (*a*) above and in addition acknowledge capital ownership as a factor which will change the shape of the indifference map and shift the demand curve to the right.

PRACTICAL APPLICATION OF INDIFFERENCE CURVE ANALYSIS

An interesting application of this analysis has been undertaken by Holm (1967),[3] using data for a medium-sized Swedish town in 1960, on the supply side taking the actual dwellings in existence, and on the demand side taking the dwellings occupied by households of various sizes, ages and incomes. He uses this analysis to study how the housing market reacts to changes in income and to changes in the number of households and is able to show the use of indifference curve type analysis to produce income consumption curves for households of different age and structure.

References

Chapter 1

1. L. Robbins, *An Essay on the Nature and Significance of Economic Science* (Macmillan, 1935)
2. K. E. Boulding, *The Skills of the Economist* (Hamish Hamilton, 1958)
3. J. M. Keynes, *The General Theory of Employment, Interest and Money* (Macmillan, 1936)
4. D. C. Hague, *Managerial Economics: Analysis for Business Decisions* (Longman, 1969)

Chapter 2

1. Department of the Environment, *Housing and Construction Statistics*, no. 1, 1st quarter, 1972, and no. 3, 3rd quarter, 1972 (H.M.S.O., 1973)
2. Central Statistical Office, *National Income and Expenditure*, 1972 (H.M.S.O., 1972)
3. Central Statistical Office, *Annual Abstract of Statistics, 1972* (H.M.S.O., 1972)
4. Building Economics Research Unit, University College Environment Research Group, 'Construction and Development: A Framework for Research and Action', paper prepared for the I.B.R.D. (London, May 1972)
5. J. Parry Lewis, *Building Cycles and Britain's Growth* (Macmillan, 1965)
6. Department of the Environment, *Annual Bulletin of Construction Statistics, 1970* (H.M.S.O., 1970)
7. P. M. Hillebrandt, 'The Capacity of the Construction Industry', to be published
8. Joint Working Party on Demand and Output Forecasts of the E.D.C.s for Building and Civil Engineering, *Construction Industry Prospects to 1979* (N.E.D.O., 1971)

Chapter 3

1. Department of the Environment, *Housing and Construction Statistics*, regular series from 1973 (H.M.S.O.)
2. Ministry of Housing and Local Government, *Housing Statistics*, regular series up to 1972 (H.M.S.O.)
3. D. Bishop, *Labour Requirements for Housebuilding: Advantages of Continuity of Work and Experience*, Building Research Station, Construction Series No. 18 (1965)
4. Department of the Environment, *Annual Bulletins and Monthly Bulletins of Construction Statistics,* regular series up to 1972
5. National Institute of Economic and Social Research, *National Institute Economic Review,* no. 60 (May 1972)
6. *Bank of England Quarterly Bulletin*, Series 1963–72
7. C. F. Carter, 'Productivity and Prices', *Building*, vol. CCXXII, no. 6733, 6 June 72, p. 68.
8. W. B. Reddaway and Associates, *Effects of the Selective Employment Tax: Final Report*, University of Cambridge, Department of Applied Economics, Occasional Paper No. 32 (Cambridge U.P., 1973)
9. W. J. Reiners, 'Cost Research', *Journal of the Royal Institution of Chartered Surveyors,* vol. xc (Sep 1957)
10. P. A. Stone, *Urban Development in Britain: Standards, Costs and Resources, 1964–2004*, vol. I: *Population Trends and Housing*, National Institute of Economic and Social Research, Economic and Social Studies, XXVI (Cambridge U.P., 1970)
11. Department of the Environment, *Housing and Construction Statistics*, no. 1, 1st quarter, 1972 (H.M.S.O., 1973)

Chapter 4

1. L. Biggeri, 'Problems of Estimation and Data Collection of Housing Quality: Proposal for a Methodology', in U.N. Economic Commission for Europe, *Housing Requirements and Demand: Current Methods of Assessment and Problems of Estimation* (Geneva: United Nations, 1973)
2. T. L. C. Duncan, *Measuring Housing Quality*, University of Birmingham, Centre for Urban and Regional Studies, Occasional Paper No. 20 (1971)

3. Colin Clark and G. T. Jones, *The Demand for Housing*, Centre for Environmental Studies, University Working Paper No. 11 (London, Sep 1971)

4. Per Holm, 'A Disaggregated Housing Market Model' in A. A. Nevitt (ed.), *The Economic Problems of Housing*, Proceedings of a Conference held by the International Economic Association (Macmillan, 1967)

5. Margaret G. Reid, *Housing and Income* (Chicago U.P., 1962)

6. M. Friedman, *A Theory of the Consumption Function* (Princeton U.P., 1957)

7. A. E. Holmans, 'A Forecast of Effective Demand for Housing in Great Britain in the 1970s', *Social Trends*, no. 1 (H.M.S.O., 1971)

8. T. L. Johnston, Lorna W. Jackson, A. Scott and P. J. Welham, *The Demand for Private Housing in Scotland*, a report for the Scottish Housing Advisory Committee (Edinburgh: H.M.S.O., 1972)

9. Joan Vipond and J. B. Walker, 'The Determinants of Housing Expenditure and Owner Occupation', *Bulletin of the Oxford University Institute of Economics and Statistics*, vol. XXXIV, no. 2 (May 1972)

10. C. M. E. Whitehead, 'A Model of the U.K. Housing Market', *Bulletin of the Oxford University Institute of Economics and Statistics*, vol. XXXIII, no. 4 (Nov 1971)

11. Assar Lindbeck, 'Rent Control as an Instrument of Housing Policy', in Nevitt (ed.), *The Economic Problems of Housing* (see ref. 4)

12. I. Stahl, 'Some Aspects of a Mixed Housing Market', in Nevitt (ed.), *The Economic Problems of Housing* (see ref. 4)

13. U.N. Economic Commission for Europe, *Studies of Effective Demand for Housing* (Geneva: United Nations, 1963)

Chapter 5

1. Department of Trade and Industry, 'Minister Gives Detailed Information on Value of Regional Incentives', *Trade and Industry*, 27 Apr 1972, p. 146

2. Joint Working Party on Demand and Output Forecasts of the E.D.C.s for Building and Civil Engineering, *Construction Industry Prospects to 1979* (N.E.D.O., 1971)

Chapter 6

1. I. M. D. Little, *A Critique of Welfare Economics* (Oxford: Clarendon Press, 1957) p. 121
2. A. R. Prest and R. Turvey, 'Cost–Benefit Analysis: A Survey', *Economic Journal*, vol. LXXV, no. 4, p. 683 (Dec 1965)
3. Economic Development Committee for Civil Engineering, *Efficiency in Road Construction* (H.M.S.O., 1966) para. 6.2
4. Malcolm Brown, 'Building was Only Half the Battle', *The Times*, M4 Supplement, 13 Jan 1972

Chapter 7

1. Central Statistical Office, *National Income and Expenditure, 1972* (H.M.S.O., 1972) Table 57
2. Building Economics Research Unit, School of Environmental Studies, University College, London, *Study of the Building Timetable: Final Report* (Dec 1971) and other reports on the same project and the Schools Consortia Study
3. Unpublished data collected for the National Economic Development Office (1972)
4. Department of the Environment, *Housing and Construction Statistics*, no. 2, 2nd quarter, 1972 (H.M.S.O., 1973)
5. M. E. A. Bowley, *The British Building Industry: Four Studies in Response and Resistance to Change* (Cambridge U.P., 1966) part IV
6. *Report of the Committee of Inquiry under Professor E. H. Phelps Brown into Certain Matters concerning Labour in Building and Civil Engineering, Research Report*, Cmnd 3714–1 (H.M.S.O., 1968)
7. Economic Development Committee for Building, *Action on the Banwell Report* (H.M.S.O., 1967)
8. Research Services Ltd, 'Labour in the Construction Industry', unpublished report prepared for the Committee of Inquiry under Professor E. H. Phelps Brown into Certain Matters concerning Labour in Building and Civil Engineering (May 1968)
9. Department of the Environment, *Housing and Construction Statistics*, no. 1, 1st quarter, 1972 (H.M.S.O., 1973)
10. Economic Development Committee for Civil Engineering,

Contracting in Civil Engineering since Banwell (H.M.S.O., 1967)

Chapter 8

1. H. Speight, *Economics and Industrial Efficiency* (Macmillan, 1967) appendix to chap. 3, pp. 73–7
2. Committee of Inquiry on Small Firms, *A Postal Questionnaire Survey of Small Firms: Non-financial Data*, Research Report No. 17 (H.M.S.O., 1972)
3. R. M. Cyert and J. G. March, *A Behavioural Theory of the Firm* (Englewood Cliffs, N.J.: Prentice-Hall, 1963)
4. D. Needham (ed.), *Readings in the Economics of Industrial Organisation* (New York: Holt, Rinehart & Winston, 1970)
5. G. P. E. Clarkson (ed.), *Managerial Economics* (Penguin Books, 1968)
6. Department of the Environment, *Housing and Construction Statistics*, no. 2, 2nd quarter, 1972 (H.M.S.O., 1973)
7. E. F. L. Brech, 'An Introduction to Management', in E. F. L. Brech (ed.), *Construction Management in Principle and Practice* (Longman, 1971), pp. 32–5
8. V. P. Gloushkov, 'New Methods of Economic Management in the U.S.S.R.: Some Features of the Recent Economic Reform', in J. Margolis and H. Guitton (eds.), *Public Economics*, Proceedings of a Conference held by the International Economic Association (Macmillan, 1969)

Chapter 9

1. Board of Trade, *Report on the Census of Production, 1963: 126, Construction* (H.M.S.O., 1969) Table 31A
2. Eleanor Lea, Peter Lansley and Paul Spencer, *Efficiency and Growth in the Building Industry: A Study of Twenty-three Building Firms*, a report of an investigation by Ashridge Management College Research Unit, sponsored by the Department of the Environment (1972); to be published
3. Research Services Ltd, 'Labour in the Construction Industry', unpublished report prepared for the Committee of Inquiry under Professor E. H. Phelps Brown into Certain Matters concerning Labour in Building and Civil Engineering (May 1968)

4. *Report of the Committee of Inquiry under Professor E. H. Phelps Brown into Certain Matters concerning Labour in Building and Civil Engineering, Research Report,* Cmnd 3714–1 (H.M.S.O., 1968)
5. Department of the Environment, *Bulletin of Construction Statistics,* supplement (Apr 1970)
6. D. A. Turin, 'The Mechanism of Response of the Construction Industry to Effective Demand: A Conceptual Framework' (Jan 1972; unpublished)
7. C. A. Smith (1955), Milton Friedman (1955) and Joe S. Bain (1954), in G. C. Archibald (ed.), *The Theory of the Firm* (Penguin Books, 1971)
8. John Halde and David Witcomb (1967), Oliver E. Williamson (1967), George J. Stigler (1958), William G. Shepheard (1967) and Stephen Hymer and Peter Pastugen (1962), in Douglas Needham (ed.), *Readings in the Economics of Industrial Organisation* (New York: Holt, Rinehart & Winston, 1970)
9. D. C. Hague, *Managerial Economics: Analysis for Business Decisions* (Longman, 1969) pp. 117–19
10. Oliver E. Williamson, 'Hierarchical Control and Optimum Firm Size' [1967], in Needham (ed.), *Readings in the Economics of Industrial Organisation* (see ref. 8)
11. D. Bishop, 'Productivity in the Building Industry', Royal Society Symposium on Building Technology in the 1980s, 4 Nov 1971

Chapter 12

1. National Joint Consultative Committee, *Code of Procedure for Selective Tendering* (R.I.B.A., 1969)
2. Joe Bain, 'A Note on Pricing in Monopoly and Oligopoly', *American Economic Review* (1949) pp. 448–64, reprinted in Richard B. Heflebower and George W. Stocking (eds.), *Readings in Industrial Organisation and Public Policy* (Homewood, Ill.: Richard D. Irwin, 1958)
3. H. Michael Mann, 'Seller Concentration, Barriers to Entry, and Rates of Return in Thirty Industries, 1950–1960', *Review of Economics and Statistics* (Aug 1966) pp. 296–307, reprinted in Douglas Needham (ed.), *Readings in the Eco-*

nomics of Industrial Organisation (New York: Holt, Rinehart & Winston, 1970)
4. M. Tamari, *A Postal Questionnaire Survey of Small Firms: An Analysis of Financial Data*, Committee of Inquiry on Small Firms, Research Report No. 16 (H.M.S.O., 1972) Table 25
5. Eleanor Lea, Peter Lansley and Paul Spencer, *Efficiency and Growth in the Building Industry: A Study of Twenty-three Building Firms*, a report of an investigation by Ashridge Management College Research Unit, sponsored by the Department of the Environment (1972); to be published

Chapter 13

1. G. L. S. Shackle, *Expectations in Economics* (Cambridge U.P., 1952)
2. F. H. Knight, *Risk, Uncertainty and Profit*, London School of Economics and Political Science Reprint No. 16 (Boston: Houghton Mifflin, 1921)
3. J. G. M. McKirdy, 'Risks in Contracting', *Building Technology and Management*, vol. ix, no. 8 (Aug 1971)
4. B. Fine and G. C. Hackemer, 'A Computer Simulation for Estimating and Bidding Strategy', unpublished paper to Conference on Decision Making for Bidding and Tendering, the City University, 20 May 1970
5. Peter H. Grinyer and John D. Whittaker, 'Management Judgement in a Competitive Bidding Model', to be published in *Operational Research Quarterly*
6. G. C. Hackemer, 'Profit and Competition, Estimating and Bidding Strategy', *Building Technology and Management*, vol. viii, no. 12 (Dec 1970) p. 617
7. Gary M. Broemser, 'Competitive Bidding in the Construction Industry', Ph.D. dissertation (Stanford University, 1968)
8. Neal B. H. Benjamin, *Competitive Bidding for Building Construction Contracts*, Technical Report No. 106, Construction Institute, Department of Civil Engineering, Stanford University (June 1969)
9. B. Fine, 'Analysis of Building Division Performance Data', unpublished paper (June 1970)
10. N. M. L. Barnes, 'On Getting Paid – the Right Amount',

paper presented to the Builders' Conference, 4 Oct 1972

11. Building Economics Research Unit, University College, London, *The Mechanism of Response to Effective Demand: Progress Report* (Nov 1972)

12. Eleanor Lea, Peter Lansley and Paul Spencer, *Efficiency and Growth in the Building Industry: A Study of Twenty-three Building Firms*, a report of an investigation by Ashridge Management College Research Unit, sponsored by the Department of the Environment (1972); to be published

13. G. L. S. Shackle, *Uncertainty in Economics* (Cambridge U.P., 1955)

14. J. B. Goodlad, 'Costing Survey', *Building*, vol. ccxxiii, no. 6752, p. 118.

15. Lawrence Friedman, 'A Competitive Bidding Strategy', *Operations Research*, vol. iv (1956) pp. 104–12

16. W. R. Park, *The Strategy of Contracting for Profit* (Englewood Cliffs, N.J.: Prentice-Hall, 1966) esp. chap. 11–15

17. W. R. Park, 'Bidders and Job Size Determine Your Optimum Mark-up', *Engineering News Record*, 20 June 1968, pp. 122–3

18. Neal B. J. Benjamin, 'Competitive Bidding; The Probability of Winning', *Journal of the Construction Division, A.S.C.E.*, vol. xcviii (Sep 1972)

19. Jack H. Willenbrock, *A Comparative Study of Expected Monetary Value and Expected Utility Value Bidding Strategy Models*, Construction Management Research Series, Report No. 3, Department of Civil Engineering, Pennsylvania State University (Mar 1972)

20. P. D. V. Marsh, *Contract Negotiation* (Gower Press, 1973)

Appendix

1. *Inland Revenue Statistics, 1972* (H.M.S.O., 1972) Tables 85–7 and notes

2. British Market Research Bureau Ltd, *Research for the Building Societies Association*, vols. i–x (B.M.R.B., 1968) or summary reports by the Building Societies Association

3. Per Holm, 'A Disaggregated Housing Market Model' in A. A. Nevitt (ed.), *The Economic Problems of Housing*, Proceedings of a Conference held by the International Economic Association (Macmillan, 1967).

Select Bibliography

Non-economists are recommended to read the relevant chapters of any good economics textbook written for degree students of economics. References to economics textbooks under chapters are therefore confined to those where the treatment of some particular subject is especially relevant.

For students requiring a general knowledge of the construction industry, the books listed under 'General Construction' are suggested. Further reading is listed under each chapter.

General Construction

M. E. A. Bowley, *The British Building Industry: Four Studies in Response and Resistance to Change* (Cambridge U.P., 1966)

Peter J. Cassimatis, *Economics of the Construction Industry* (New York: National Industrial Conference Board, 1969)

J. R. Colclough, *The Construction Industry of Great Britain* (Butterworth, 1965)

P. M. Hillebrandt, *Small Firms in the Construction Industry*, Committee of Inquiry on Small Firms, Research Report No. 10 (H.M.S.O., 1971)

Malcolm Hislop, 'The Industry and the Market', 'The Industry and the Professions' and 'Development of the Industry', in E. F. L. Brech (ed.), *Construction Management in Principle and Practice* (Longman, 1971)

H. W. Richardson and Derek H. Aldcroft, *Building in the British Economy between the Wars* (Allen & Unwin, 1968)

P. A. Stone, *Building Economy: Design, Production and Organisation – a Synoptic View* (Pergamon Press, 1966)

Selected Bibliography by Chapter

Chapter 1

Kenneth E. Boulding, *The Skills of the Economist* (Hamish Hamilton, 1958)

Milton Friedman, 'The Methodology of Positive Economics', in William Breit and Harold M. Hochman (eds.), *Readings in Microeconomics* (New York: Holt, Rinehart & Winston, 1969)

D. C. Hague, *Managerial Economics: Analysis for Business Decisions* (Longman, 1969) introduction and chapter 1

L. Robbins, *An Essay on the Nature and Significance of Economic Science* (Macmillan, 1935)

D. A. Turin, *What Do We Mean by Building?*, Inaugural lecture, University College, London (1966)

J. Wilczynski, *The Economics of Socialism* (Allen & Unwin, 1970). For profit under capitalism and under socialism, see pp. 55–8

Alan Williams, *Output Budgeting and the Contribution of Microeconomics to Efficiency in Government*, C. A. S. Occasional Papers No. 4 (H.M.S.O., 1967)

Chapter 2

J. Parry Lewis, *Building Cycles and Britain's Growth* (Macmillan, 1965)

J. Parry Lewis and D. D. Singh, 'Government Policy and the Building Industry', *District Bank Review*, no. 158 (June 1966)

J. Parry Lewis, *Population, the Labour Force and Building, 1968–1990*, Dewe Rogerson Occasional Paper No. 1 (Sep 1969)

H. W. Richardson and Derek H. Aldcroft, *Building in the British Economy between the Wars* (Allen & Unwin, 1968)

P. A. Stone, *Building Economy* (Pergamon Press, 1966) pp. 1–28

Chapter 3

D. C. Hague, *Managerial Economics: Analysis for Business Decisions* (Longman, 1969) chap. 5, 'Costs'

H. Speight, *Economics and Industrial Efficiency* (Macmillan, 1967) chap. 1

P. A. Stone, *Building Economy* (Pergamon Press, 1966) chaps. 1, 2, 3, 7 and 15

U.N. Economic Commission for Europe, *Multi-level Planning and Decision Making*, papers presented to the Sixth Meeting of Senior Economic Advisers to the E.C.E. Governments, Report No. E/ECE/750 (New York: United Nations, 1970) esp. background paper on 'Opportunity Cost', etc.

Chapter 4

C. Buchanan and Partners, *The Prospect for Housing*, a study for the Nationwide Building Society (1971)

I. C. R. Byatt, A. E. Holmans and D. E. W. Laidler, 'Income and the Demand for Housing: Some Evidence for Great Britain', in M. Parkin with A. R. Nobay (ed.), *Essays in Modern Economics: The Proceedings of the Association of University Teachers of Economics, Aberystwyth 1972* (Longman, 1973)

Colin Clark and G. T. Jones, *The Demand for Housing*, Centre for Environmental Studies, University Working Paper No. 11 (London, Sep 1971)

D. V. Donnison, *The Government of Housing* (Penguin Books, 1967)

A. E. Holmans, 'A Forecast of Effective Demand for Housing in Great Britain in the 1970s', *Social Trends*, no. 1 (H.M.S.O., 1970) pp. 33–42

Joint Working Party on Demand and Output Forecasts of the E.D.C.s for Building and Civil Engineering, *Construction Industry Prospects to 1979* (N.E.D.O., 1971)

R. M. Kirwan and D. B. Martin, *The Economic Basis for Models of the Housing Market*, Centre for Environmental Studies, Working Paper No. 62 (London, May 1970)

I. M. D. Little, *A Critique of Welfare Economics* (Oxford: Clarendon Press, 1957) chaps. 1–3

L. Needleman, *The Economics of Housing* (Staples Press, 1965)

A. A. Nevitt (ed.), *The Economic Problems of Housing*, Proceedings of a Conference held by the International Economic Association (Macmillan, 1967)

U.N. Economic Commission for Europe, *Housing Requirements and Demand: Current Methods of Assessment and Problems of Estimation* (Geneva: United Nations, 1973)

R. K. Wilkinson with S. Gulliver, 'Economics of Housing', *Social and Economic Administration*, vol. 5, no. 2 (April 1971) p. 83

Chapter 5

Joint Working Party on Demand and Output Forecasts of the E.D.C.s for Building and Civil Engineering, *Construction Industry Prospects to 1979* (N.E.D.O., 1971) pp. 119–54

A. D. Knox, 'The Acceleration Principle and the Theory of Investment: A Survey', in M. G. Mueller (ed.), *Readings in Macroeconomics* (New York: Holt, Rinehart & Winston, 1969)

William W. White, 'Interest Inelasticity of Investment Demand: The Case from Business Attitude Surveys Re-examined', in Mueller (ed.), *Readings in Macroeconomics*

Chapter 6

Joint Working Party on Demand and Output Forecasts of the E.D.C.s for Building and Civil Engineering, *Construction Industry Prospects to 1979* (N.E.D.O., 1971) pp. 71–118

I. M. D. Little, *A Critique of Welfare Economics* (Oxford: Clarendon Press, 1957)

J. Margolis and H. Guitton (eds.), *Public Economics*, Proceedings of a Conference held by the International Economic Association (Macmillan, 1969) esp. J. Margolis's introduction and R. A. Musgrave, 'Provision for Social Goods'

P. A. Stone, *Urban Development in Britain: Standards, Costs and Resources, 1964–2004*, vol. I: *Population Trends and Housing*, National Institute of Economic and Social Research, Economic and Social Studies, XXVI (Cambridge U.P., 1970)

H. G. Walsh and Alan Williams, *Current Issues in Cost–Benefit Analysis*, C.A.S. Occasional Papers No. 11 (H.M.S.O., 1969)

Alan Williams, *Output Budgeting and the Contribution of Microeconomics to Efficiency in Government*, C.A.S. Occasional Papers No. 4 (H.M.S.O., 1967)

D. M. Winch, *Analytical Welfare Economics* (Penguin Books, 1971)

Chapter 7

Malcolm Hislop and A. Miller, 'Control of Incoming Work', in E. F. L. Brech (ed.), *Construction Management in Principle and Practice* (Longman, 1971)

Chapter 8

W. J. Baumol, *Economic Theory and Operations Analysis* (Englewood Cliffs, N.J.: Prentice-Hall, 1965) chap. 13, 'The Firm and its Objectives'

G. P. E. Clarkson (ed.), *Managerial Economics* (Penguin Books, 1968) esp. for H. A. Simon (1959), 'Theories of Decision-making in Economics and Behavioural Science', and others

R. M. Cyert and J. G. March, *A Behavioural Theory of the Firm* (Englewood Cliffs, N.J.: Prentice-Hall, 1963)

Douglas Needham (ed.), *Readings in the Economics of Industrial Organisation* (New York: Holt, Rinehart & Winston, 1970) esp. part I, 'Firms' Objectives', with articles by Fritz Machling, William L. Baldwin, John Williamson and Ezra Solomon

Chapter 9

G. C. Archibald (ed.), *The Theory of the Firm* (Penguin Books, 1971); relevant papers on costs

M. E. A. Bowley, *The British Building Industry* (Cambridge U.P., 1966) part III

Peter J. Cassimatis, *Economics of the Construction Industry* (New York: National Industrial Conference Board, 1969)

D. C. Hague, *Managerial Economics* (Longman, 1969), chap. 5, pp. 102–21

Douglas Needham (ed.), *Readings in the Economics of Industrial Organisation* (New York: Holt, Rinehart & Winston, 1970); section on costs

C. F. Pratten, *Economies of Scale in Manufacturing Industry*, University of Cambridge, Department of Applied Economics, Occasional Paper No. 28 (Cambridge U.P., 1971)

Chapter 13

Neal B. H. Benjamin, *Competitive Bidding for Building Construction Contracts*, Technical Report No. 106, Construction

Institute, Department of Civil Engineering, Stanford University (June 1969)

Alan Coddington, *Theories of the Bargaining Process*, Studies in Economics No. 2 (Allen & Unwin, 1968)

P. D. V. Marsh, *Contract Negotiation* (Gower Press, 1973)

W. R. Park, *The Strategy of Contracting for Profit* (Englewood Cliffs, N.J.: Prentice-Hall, 1966)

G. L. S. Shackle, *Expectations in Economics* (Cambridge U.P., 1952)

M. G. Wright, G. C. Hackemer, A. B. Moore, P. D. V. Marsh, G. J. J. Hunt, L. G. Bayley, John Andrews and Denis Harper, 'The Strategy of Contracting for Profit', special issue of *Building Technology and Management*, vol. VIII, no. 12 (Dec 1970)

Index

Definitions and discussions of the use of terms are shown in bold type. The following abbreviations are used:

f   figure
n   footnote
t   table